Joseph,

Enjoy this book about
a great man and wonderful
priest.

Fr. David G Morman

AN ORDINARY
DISCIPLE
OF CHRIST

Front Cover

Father William J. Fahnlander counsels a boy under the watchful
gaze of Home on the Range for Boys founder Father Elwood Cassedy
in this October 1962 picture.

(Photo by Bismarck Tribune staff photographer Leo LaLonde;
from Home On The Range archives.)

AN ORDINARY
DISCIPLE
OF CHRIST

FR. WILLIAM J.
FAHNLANDER

Edited by
Rev. David G. Morman
and Jeri L. Dobrowski

With a foreword by
Most Reverend Paul A. Zipfel,
Bishop of Bismarck

An Ordinary Disciple of Christ

Copyright 2002 By
Rev. David G. Morman
&
Jeri L. Dobrowski

ISBN: 0-9718139-0-6

First Printing of 5,000 copies: March 2002

Published By
Rev. David G. Morman
Pastor, Church of St. John the Baptist
PO Box 337
Beach, ND 58621
(701) 872-4153

Printed By
Fine Print of Grand Forks, Inc.
PO Box 5358
Grand Forks, ND 58206
(701) 772-4802

Contents

Editor's Notes

Home on the Range for Boys was the legal name of the benevolent, educational corporation first registered with the State of North Dakota on December 28, 1949. Most Reverend Vincent J. Ryan, Bishop of Bismarck; Monsignor J.J. Raith, Vicar General of the Diocese of Bismarck; Father Elwood E. Cassedy; T. Clem Casey; and Ray Schnell were the original incorporators.

In August 1990, after 40 years of serving only boys, the doors were opened to female residents. To accommodate the change in population, the official name was shortened to Home On The Range.

Both versions of the Ranch's name appear within the stories and letters included in this compilation. Every effort was made to use the names as consistently as possible, indicating the time frame of the reference, while at the same time acknowledging each contributor's own personal usage. "Boys' Ranch" and "The Ranch" have also been used through the years in reference to Home On The Range.

Home On The Range does not receive financial support from the Bismarck Catholic Diocese. Care rates charged for services cover approximately 75 percent of the actual cost. The remainder must be raised through gifts of cash and assets, the agricultural operation, grants, fund raising events, and investments. The Ranch is a recognized 501(c)(3) organization. Contributions are fully tax deductible in accordance with IRS regulations.

Profits from the sale of this book are being donated to the Father Fahnlander Endowment at Home On The Range. This fund was established in Father Bill's name to support the religious programming at the Ranch. Donations may be sent to:

Fr. Fahnlander Endowment
Home On The Range
16351 I-94
Sentinel Butte, ND 58654
701-872-3745

Acknowledgements

I am indebted to Jeri Dobrowski for her untiring work in gathering material and organizing it in such a way that makes this book a pleasure to read. Also, I would like to thank Father Fahnlander's niece Mary Jo Norum and Wanda Olson of Home On The Range, whose assistance made this book possible.

Rev. David G. Morman

This collection of stories is the brainchild of Rev. David Morman. He first suggested the idea of honoring Father Fahnlander, in book form, to me on March 31, 2001. We were atop Cassedy Hill at Home On The Range, bracing ourselves against a strong and biting wind. Grave side services for Father Fahnlander had just concluded. I thank Father David for the opportunity to be involved with a project that has been inspiring, challenging, entertaining, comforting, and thought provoking.

My deepest thanks to Father Fahnlander's family and friends who responded when we solicited personal stories about him and what made him so divinely special. Darrell Dorgan's video footage of an interview with Father Fahnlander was indispensable in preparing the first three chapters. Fraternal Order of Eagles members Pete Ehrmann, Linda Heffner, and Bill Loffer dug through photos and archives of the Grand Aerie, providing details about Father Fahnlander's long and colorful association with the Eagles. I tip my hat to Wanda Olson and Marge Grosz, the two best proof readers I could ask for. Lastly, thanks to Amy LaFontaine and Fine Print of Grand Forks, N. Dak., who masterfully transformed my computer files and pages of instructions into the book you are now holding. Many hands *truly* do make light work.

Jeri L. Dobrowski

Summer in the North Dakota Bad Lands.
(Photo courtesy of Fahnlander Family.)

Preface

Solemnity of the Epiphany
January 6, 2002

A week before he died, Father Fahnlander told me that he had been named as one of Saint Paul Seminary's Distinguished Alumni for 2001. With his characteristic meekness, he stated, "What did I do to deserve such recognition?"

In the pages that follow you will read stories by people who knew and loved Father Bill. You will see an extraordinary human being and a gracious priest, a man I count as one of my heroes.

In reading about Father Fahnlander's life and ministry, my hope is that you will come to a deeper realization of the truly good people who grace your life. People, who by the way they live their lives, manifest something of the presence of God. I believe that God grants us such people to encourage and to inspire us so that we will become better people ourselves.

"He was the most Christlike person I have ever met," were words used by Mary Jo Norum to describe her beloved uncle. These words portray a Christian and a priest whose life was well-lived. This would be my prayer for each of you who read this book.

Rev. David G. Morman
Pastor, St. John the Baptist
Beach, North Dakota

*The colored sunsets and
starry heavens,
the beautiful mountains and
the shining seas,
the fragrant woods and
painted flowers,
are not half so beautiful
as a soul that
is serving Jesus out of love,
in the wear and tear
of common, unpoetic life.*

— Fr. Frederick W. Faber
1814-1863

Foreword

Every now and then someone comes along who touches our life in a special way. Father William Fahnlander was such a person for many who knew him.

What are the qualities of this priest that gave him such a great impact with young and old, rich and poor, troubled and confident, learned and unlearned?

The first quality: Father Bill was a man of joy. People who saw him, heard him, and touched him knew that he enjoyed his priesthood and that it was the most important aspect in his life. People sensed his peace and joy as a priest and they simply enjoyed being with him. His every word, every gesture, every look said, "I'm delighted to be here, delighted to be with you." This was true not only at the altar, but when counseling a troubled youngster, attending a board meeting, visiting in the hospital, or helping at a fund raiser. Surely there were many youngsters who looked at him and said, "That's what I want to be like when I grow old."

The second quality: Father Bill was a humble man. He was a man for others. He never seemed to put himself at the center of the story. Although he received many awards for his accomplishments over the years, he never pointed to his trophies as if he deserved to stand on a level above anyone else. Like Jesus, he became increasingly aware of his solidarity with every man and every woman. He was aware of his sameness with others, which made him laugh with joy and be able to say with Thomas Merton: "Thank God, thank God that I am like other men, that I am only a man among others." By keeping his feet on the level of every brother and sister, he could share the hungers of each person he knew and become their servant.

The third quality: Father Bill was a man of prayer; he knew the person of Jesus. He responded to Jesus' invitation to "come and see" the place of God. Father Bill moved hearts because it was evident to people that he was fired by the presence of Jesus whom he found in the Word, the assembly, as well as the blessed bread and wine. His experience of the living God was so rich that it could not be imprisoned. He found himself telling others, with and without words, that he loved God with all his soul and strength. His communion with Jesus spilled over into everything he said and did.

A man of joy. A humble man. A man of prayer. Is it any wonder that he touched hearts?

Thank you, Father Bill, for being one of the most Christlike priests that many have ever known.

Most Reverend Paul A. Zipfel
Bishop of Bismarck
Bismarck, North Dakota

The Best Way to Live is...

To trust the Lord

To keep peace in one's heart

To accept all things as being for the best

To be patient and good

Never to do ill.

— Pope John XXIII

CHAPTER ONE

Faithful is He

It was with reluctance that I took over Father Cassedy's work (at Home on the Range for Boys). I had wanted to be a parish priest – and – only considered this temporary until someone else could be found for this work. Little by little, the boys "converted" me. In March 1959, I gave up the parish and went into this full time and with the desire to give all I could to it. The satisfaction of seeing boys – who might well have become delinquents, for lack of a decent chance – turn out good, has proved to be a most rewarding work.

— Comment added by Father Fahnlander
to bottom of a biographical sketch

To have seen Father William Fahnlander at the helm of Home On The Range from March 1959 until his death in March 2001, it would have been hard to imagine a time when he wasn't wholly devoted to the children living there. There wasn't a more jubilant papa anywhere in the world, nor a dad who hurt as deeply, when it came to Father Fahnlander and "his boys," as he so often called them. Jubilation when a Bismarck boy he helped raise was named Maryland Teacher of the Year, dejection when another ended up in prison.

"Each one of these kids, when they leave, they take a piece of your heart with 'em," said Fahnlander in a November 1998 interview with journalist Darrell Dorgan. "Back when I was just filling in, one boy asked another why he always called me 'Father.' He turned to me and said, 'You're the only dad I got, ain't ya, Father?' We had a closeness back then and they were just like one of yours. It hurt when they didn't measure up. If he got hurt, it hurt you, too.

"I hear from the boy in Maryland every couple months. He and another boy in the construction business, we keep in touch regularly. The contractor's doing well, has a family. He keeps talking about Home On The Range

William Joseph Fahnlander, born
February 27, 1921, the son of William Peter
and Mildred (Lorenz) Fahnlander, Minot, N. Dak.
(Photo courtesy of Fahnlander Family.)

and wonders where he'd be without it. They tell me, 'Thanks for teaching us to work!' Work is a therapy. That's why we had five thousand laying hens plus the dairy. The kids felt a part of it, felt responsibility."

Fahnlander remembers listening to the kids at the breakfast table arguing which helped the ranch more, the dairy crew or the chicken crew. They had a feeling of ownership in the tasks to which they were assigned because to them the ranch was "home" (Dakota Catholic Action, 2000).

"Home On The Range served the homeless and neglected in the early years," Fahnlander explained. "Human Services is doing the job of placing orphans now. Today kids at the Ranch have problems. They have been ticketed to go down the tube if not for a place like ours."

Although not technically an orphan, young Billy Fahnlander knew what it felt like to grow up without a father: "Both my parents were from the Osnabrock, North Dakota, area up near Langdon. They were married in Grand Forks in 1911 and moved to Minot shortly thereafter. Dad was a tailor downtown in Minot. He built new over on 3rd Street Northeast. I attended Lincoln School for the first grade, then started second grade over at St. Leo's when my folks moved to the new plant with an apartment upstairs.

"I was in the third grade when Dad died. Mother had a fifth grade education and knew nothing about running a business. The Depression hit right after she took over. She thought Governor Bill Langer was the greatest, he imposed a moratorium on all foreclosures and she paid it off."

Raised by his devoutly Catholic mother who immigrated from Germany during World War I, Billy found a mentor and second dad in the person of Rev. John W. Hogan. Hogan served Minot's Church of St. Leo from 1923 until his death in 1959. Rounding out the family was Eloise, Billy Fahnlander's sister, nine years his senior.

Sports, school, and work were young Bill's life. "We used to play a lot of basketball when I was growing up. We'd go to service stations and get their used oil to blacktop my best friend's backyard court," he said.

Writing in St. Leo's 100th anniversary publication, "St. Leo's: The First 100 Years (1886-1986)," he added, "Hanging around the school office, shooting baskets in the gym and playing ping pong in the office were favorite pastimes of many of us. He (Father Hogan) allowed that office to be more of a teen center than an office."

St. Leo's winning Lions of 1939: Father Hogan coached St. Leo's to the North Dakota State Class B Basketball championship in 1938 & 1939. Guard Bill Fahnlander, wearing the number "3" on his purple and white uniform, helped give St. Leo's their first state basketball crown in 1938. The Lions conquered Stanley (32-27) in the finals. The wiry, fleet-footed Fahnlander was named to the second string all state basketball team that year. St. Leo's retained their Class B title in 1939, beating Lakota. Back row, standing: Dominic Pouliot; Eloy Charlebois; Edward Claussen; Mark DeMots; Clarence Gavett; Gerald Callahan. Front row, sitting: Edward Brockwell; Walter Tooley; Lyle King; William Fahnlander.
(Photo courtesy of Fahnlander Family.)

Father Hogan coached the St. Leo's Lions to the North Dakota State Class B Basketball championship in 1938 & 1939. Guard Bill Fahnlander, wearing the number "3" on his purple and white uniform, helped give St. Leo's their first state basketball crown in 1938. The Lions conquered Stanley (32-27) in the finals. Hardly a newspaper article was written that year that didn't mention Bill Fahnlander in regard to his abilities on the floor. The wiry, fleet-footed Fahnlander was named to the second string all state basketball team that year.

St. Leo's retained their Class B title in 1939, beating Lakota. Students enjoyed a vacation from classes to celebrate their team's victory.

During Father Hogan's reign as basketball coach at St. Leo's (1933 to 1943), he amassed an impressive record of 167 wins, 41 losses, and 3 state championships. The third would come in 1943. His fellow coaches proclaimed it the best record ever achieved in a decade of coaching (St. Leo's: The First 100 Years, 1986). Reflecting on his coach's winning technique years later, Father Bill commented, "I don't know how much basketball he knew. But, he knew when we needed a kick in the pants or a pat on the back!"

Bananas were selling 3 pounds for 23 cents and lettuce 2 heads for 17 cents, when Bill set two track records his senior year. Participating at the Mouse River Loop Conference Track and Field Meet, he recorded a time of 5 minutes, 11 seconds in the mile and 2:16.2 in the half-mile. He also was a member of the relay team which won the half-mile relay with a time of 1:47.8.

Following commencement exercises in the spring of 1939, the St. Leo's class valedictorian competed at the North Dakota Interscholastic Track and Field Meet in Grand Forks. He placed third in the mile run.

"Glenn Cunningham, the great miler, was my hero. He had been crippled when he was burned in a schoolhouse fire." Cunningham defied doctors who said that he would never walk again. Competing in collegiate and Olympic events, he earned the nickname "Kansas Ironman." In 1934 he set the world's record of 4:06 in the mile. "I wanted to run the mile like him," said Bill.

Lamenting the lack of a track coach for all but his senior year, Bill figured he might have placed higher given a more lengthy and sophisticated preparation. As it was, his most consistent training method came during the lunch hour when he and a friend would run home for lunch. It was a mile

High school basketball standout Billy Fahnlander
lettered for his accomplishments on the court.
Hardly a newspaper article about the Lions was
written in 1938 that didn't mention Bill Fahnlander
in regard to his abilities on the floor.
(Photo courtesy of Fahnlander Family.)

each way, and they made the trip every day. There was no hot lunch program offered in the school with an enrollment of 140 students.

Aside from sports, there wasn't a wide offering of activities at St. Leo's School in the '30s. There were student council and dramatics, and the young Fahnlander once played a crook in a school play. Playing the role of Limpy Lanigan, he admittedly botched his lines. And, there was the annual prom. The popular young lad was named king three years running, despite his theatrical shortcomings.

When Bill wasn't hanging out at Father Hogan's office, practicing his moves on the hardwood, or dancing with the girls, he was helping his mother at the dry-cleaning plant. He spoke with admiration of his mother's role in managing the family business following his father's death.

With characteristic humor, Bill said he brushed lint out of the cuffs and pockets of garments at the plant, pressed pants, and delivered clothes – all the while trying to decide whether he'd dry-clean clothes or souls for the rest of his life. "I struggled with the idea of becoming a priest all the way through to the end," he conceded to Dorgan. "It was not unusual for a guy to become a priest when I was growing up. Father Hogan was a great recruiter, and some of the sisters pegged me for it and were praying for me. Monsignor William Garvin spent summers when he was in the seminary driving delivery truck for the plant. I rode around with him when I was little.

"I like to think I was kinda halfway normal. In college I dated a girl from St. Ben's, which was near St. John's. I was studying Latin and Greek at the time. The other guys at a dance gave me grief (for going out with a girl)."

Nineteen young men from St. Leo's were ordained priests, influenced by the example of Father Hogan, who was later invested as a monsignor. How pleased he must have been to see these 19 young men profess vocations. The monsignor had yet another reason to be delighted by his former students: Bill Fahnlander and five of his classmates took to the basketball court at St. John's University. An article and photo in the January 9, 1941, *Minot Daily News* touted:

> "Here Are The Johnnies From Minot"… It's not often that six boys from one city are members of a college basketball team, but here are six former St. Leo's cagers from Minot who are representing the Magic City on the St. John's

Billy Fahnlander's senior picture - 1939.
He served as class president all four years of
high school and graduated as valedictorian.
(Photo from Home On The Range archives.)

University quints of Collegeville, Minn., this season. In the front row, left to right, are Eloy Charlebois, Captain Ed Claussen and Pat Freuen. In the back are Joe Adkins, Walt Tooley and Bill Fahnlander...

Characterized by Rev. Albert Leary, Father Hogan was a dedicated and devoted pastor: "He taught me much that was good and useful about being a priest. He had an engaging personality which made him a popular community figure and he had brains and guts which made him capable of handling difficult situations quite well" (St. Leo's: The First 100 Years, 1986).

In the section entitled "The Hogan Years 1923-1959," the man who was a mentor for so many future priests is lovingly remembered:

Basketball was only one part of Father Hogan's life at St. Leo's. He tried to be all things to his students, bringing into their Catholic world in the little school a smattering of what life was all about. Those early years in the school were the Depression years, so no one had any money. Certainly, none of the students had cars. But Father Hogan did, and he shared his capacity for fun and mischief with the students.

Periodically, the call would go out, 'Father Hogan's going swimming!' It would be early spring, the weather one of those unseasonably warm days when being in school was unbearable and being outdoors was imperative. He'd load up his Model T Coupe. Its capacity probably was six, counting the driver. Only he'd wind up with as many as 23 kids (they were counted once), and they'd head out to Burlington or Puppy Dog, the car a moving mass of humanity...

He took students on baseball and football trips. He organized baseball teams to "give the kids some recreation..." He kept the teams going by begging, borrowing or stealing what was needed.

He taught classes in religion and psychology, although it often was hard for students to differentiate between the two. Each seemed like a mix of the other, and any texts that were used were secondary to whatever he espoused...

Father Fahnlander officiating at marriage of his sister
Eloise to Elmer (Bucky) Meyer, August 31, 1946. Father Bill witnessed
the ceremony, his first, at the Church of St. Leo, Minot.
(Photo courtesy of Fahnlander Family.)

Just because a student graduated or left St. Leo's, his or her relationship with Father Hogan wasn't necessarily over. He was known to keep in contact with former students via mail. His letters took on the flavor of an old and dear friend rather than that of the jovial but demanding cleric they had previously known.

World War II was being fought while Bill Fahnlander prepared for the priesthood. "I was in college, and my friends were going into the service. I came awfully close to dropping out and enlisting. I thought I could come back after the war. Father Hogan, himself a St. Paul alum, and the priests at the seminary told me they needed chaplains, so I stayed put. I had four years of college and four of theology."

Proud family members gathered in 1943 when Bill graduated from St. John's University, Collegeville, Minn. He then attended and graduated from Saint Paul Seminary, St. Paul, Minn.

Billy Fahnlander was ordained Father William J. Fahnlander on June 11, 1946, at the Cathedral of the Holy Spirit, Bismarck, N. Dak., by Most Reverend Vincent J. Ryan. He witnessed his first marriage, that of his sister Eloise to Elmer Meyer, at St. Leo's on August 31, 1946.

Father Fahnlander's first assignment was as a junior assistant at St. Mary's in Bismarck. Telling Dorgan, he said, "I was there for six months. It was a delightful six months. I was there with Father Blaine Cook. He coached. I coached. But, there was a need in Minot for a priest with school credentials. At that time they had all priests and sisters teaching. One priest was in poor health, having had a kidney removed, and they needed me there."

The reassignment was a crushing blow to the young priest. In those days it was unheard of to be moved after such a short time – unless the priest was especially disliked. Bishop Ryan assured the fledgling priest that was not the case. Rather, it was because of his training in education that he was being moved, to fill a position at St. Leo's School, his alma mater.

A second wave of dread swept over Father Fahnlander as he envisioned himself standing in front of his home parish where people knew him as Billy Fahnlander. He pondered the parishioners' reactions as he looked over the assembly on Sunday morning: seeing guys he ran around with in high school, girls he dated, and people who watched him grow up. "I was really self-conscious being in my parish for the first two years," he commented.

Father Bill unpacked his belongings in the St. Leo's rectory in February

Father Fahnlander was the guest of honor at a birthday party assembly at St. Leo's on February 26, 1954. The entire student body and faculty sang "Happy Birthday," followed by a skit, violin solo, and other entertainment, all taking place on the school's stage. The afternoon culminated with the cutting of the cake. Here Father Bill is joined by his mother Mildred.

(Photo courtesy of Fahnlander Family.)

1947. His assignment as an assistant pastor included teaching in the grade and high school, coaching basketball, pastoral duties at the Church of St. Leo and the Church of St. Philomena, Glenburn, and assistant chaplain duties at the Minot Veterans Administration Hospital. In 1950 he was named St. Leo's High School principal, a position once held by his former basketball coach and mentor, Father Hogan.

Working from dawn until dusk would have been easier than working for Father Hogan, who expected his young staff to also possess his nearly super-human stamina. Summing up his experience as an assistant to Father Hogan, Rev. Albert Leary painted the following picture in "Interim 1959:"

> Monsignor Hogan never allowed us to have any time off. He set a frantic pace himself most of the time – I believed him to be a workaholic – and he demanded the same of us... Getting up at 5:00 a.m. to get ready for the convent Mass, it was not at all uncommon to climb the stairs at 10:00 p.m. or later, to take the first real breather of the day. More than once I looked in on Father Schneider who would be on his knees by the side of his bed, sound asleep, with night prayers still unfinished.
>
> I can remember in those days – the days of the old Latin liturgy – we used to have to turn from the altar and face the congregation and say "Dominus Vobiscum." I remember turning and having to hold onto the altar to prevent myself from falling. I literally couldn't do it. I thought I might have a brain tumor or something like that since I was losing my balance at times. I went to Dr. Hurley who examined me thoroughly and announced, 'There is nothing wrong with you. You don't have a brain tumor. You are simply exhausted!'"

That was the life of an assistant at St. Leo's in the pre-Vatican II days. Rules at the rectory were strict and we could do nothing without official authorization from Monsignor Hogan. One could not leave the rectory at night to go to a movie without his explicit permission... He was difficult to work for because he seemed to expect always more than one thought humanly possible (St. Leo's: The First

100 Years, 1986).

In typical judicious form, Father Fahnlander summarized his eight years under Hogan's puritanical administration:

> From the second grade on through high school, I attended St. Leo's. I had the tremendous experience of growing up under Father Hogan, becoming a priest and then serving under him in that capacity for 8½ years. I like to think that I saw him at his best and at his worst. He often said, 'I would rather be respected than liked.' He stepped on toes. I know a lot of people who hated his guts, but in the end, he was the guy they ran to for help. To me he was a genius with his feet on the ground, an eminently practical man (St. Leo's: The First 100 Years, 1986).

In August 1955, Father Fahnlander was granted a long-held wish, the chance to become a pastor. He was assigned to shepherd the Church of St. Michael in Sentinel Butte, N. Dak., with its mission, the Church of St. Mary at Medora. There was one small catch: with the assignment came part-time superintendent duties at the nearby Home on the Range for Boys. The ranch home, owned by the Bismarck Diocese and operated by Father Elwood Cassedy, cared for orphaned and neglected boys. Heading off to the western part of the state may have gladdened the young Fahnlander, but it dismayed a large portion of Minot.

A report by Tom Miller appearing in the August 24, 1955, *Minot Daily News* said it best:

> "Sentiment Runs High As Parishioners, Friends Bid Goodbye To "Their Father Bill"
>
> The truth of the statement that the worth of an individual isn't fully realized until he is about to leave was brought home with striking force last night when a large group of Minot citizens gathered to pay tribute and say their goodbyes to a community and church leader.
>
> The indifferent observer could not help but be touched by the display of emotion exhibited in the clubrooms of St.

Leo's Catholic Church when parishioners of both St. Leo's and Little Flower churches and many non-Catholic friends from all walks of life shook hands with "their Father Bill" – the Rev. William J. Fahnlander – and wished him well in his new assignment at Sentinel Butte.

Some of them were saying goodbye to a parish priest and school principal... others to a man who, through athletics, educational work and youth activities, had done much to support community projects... and still others who remembered the priest from the days of his boyhood when kids kicked tin cans down the street, played sandlot sports, served Mass as an altar boy and did all of the things every lively boy does in the years of growing to maturity.

This was the case of a hometown boy who made good in his hometown, rising from average beginnings to become a leader in his community.

Here was a man who, in his high school days, was noted throughout the state as a whirling dervish on the basketball court. Smaller than average for the court game, he made up for his size by his alertness and speed and bounce – made up for it to such an extent that he was named to the all state Class B squad two years in a row.

But some time during his growing years he turned from the material things of the world and devoted himself to his church with the same intentness he had formerly devoted to sports...

His return to his hometown as a man was more of a marked event than would have been true of a person coming back to establish a successful business career. In this case, he returned to a position of authority that transcended worldly things. As a layman might put it, he became a "middleman between his parishioners and God."

And they respected this man whom they had known as a boy – not only those who were younger than he, but also those many others who remembered him as a basketball scrapper, as a normal boy.

Often it is the case that after a person leaves his surround-

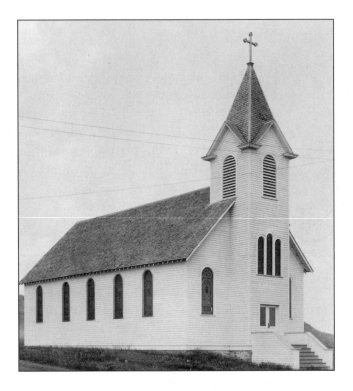

Church of St. Michael and rectory, Sentinel Butte, N. Dak.
(Photo courtesy of Bismarck Catholic Diocese.)

ings, those left behind bewail the missed opportunity in not saying their goodbyes in a way which would reflect their feelings and sentiments. Not so last night in the case of "Father Bill."

When Father Fahnlander made his entrance with other parish priests, the clubrooms were crowded. It was a quiet meeting – befitting this quiet man, who was described as a "humble man" and a "man's man" by one of a number of parishioners who spoke briefly...

Though the saying is trite, one of the speakers seemed to sum up the sentiments of those present when he said, "We can't be selfish; we've had Father Fahnlander for 8½ years; Minot's loss is Sentinel Butte's gain."

Settling in at St. Michael's old two-story rectory, in the pint-sized municipality of Sentinel Butte, Father Fahnlander was at long last, a priest in charge of his own congregation. What a change it was, however, from the hustle and bustle associated with St. Leo's lavishly redecorated expanses. St. Michael's modest church proper had been constructed in large part by donated labor of the congregation. Bishop Vincent Wehrle, O.S.B., dedicated the structure, with a final price tag of $2,820, on October 10, 1915. St. Michael's hadn't even been a fully functioning parish until 1948, when Father Laurence Talty was assigned. Up until that point it had been served sporadically by pastors from nearby St. John's in Beach (Golden Valley County Pioneers, 1976). Nonetheless, it was his parish, and the first one he could call his own in the nine years since his ordination.

Father Fahnlander set about fulfilling his parish and mission duties, as well as lending a hand at Father Cassedy's Home on the Range for Boys. He joined three other staff members there: a ranch foreman, a repairman/barber/counselor, and a retired nurse who also served as cook and secretary to Cassedy. Home on the Range for Boys was located 4½ miles northwest of Sentinel Butte. St. Mary's in Medora, a quaint brick chapel, had been built in 1884 by the aristocratic Marquis de Mores for his wife, Medora. It was a 13-mile journey to the east to serve his flock there.

CHAPTER TWO
Seeking God's Will

The story of Home on the Range for Boys began in 1949 with another Catholic priest, Father Elwood E. Cassedy. Cassedy always denied that he was trying to build a second Father Flanagan's Boys' Town (Newsweek, 1951). He simply wanted to save neglected and homeless boys and thought "a ranch, complete with cattle, horses and all that would delight the average American boy." Cassedy had seen first hand the effects induced by neglect and homelessness as he traveled the streets of New York City during the 1920s. Cassedy was the oldest child in his family and after completing the eighth grade, found employment as a page for the Equitable Trust Company. Working to help support his family, Cassedy saw boys near his own age who were living on the streets. He watched them fight, steal, and gamble to get food, clothing, or a place to sleep. Many formed gangs and became threats to society.

Following graduation from Notre Dame University and the seminary, Cassedy was ordained in 1944 as a priest for the Bismarck Diocese. In 1949, Rev. Cassedy, a member of the Fraternal Order of Eagles, was asked to address an Eagles convention in Deadwood, S. Dak., regarding the problems of youth. During his presentation he made mention of his long-held dream to start a boys' ranch. A spontaneous collection at the conclusion of his speech netted $123. It was very fortunate that the *Bismarck Tribune* carried the story reporting Cassedy's dream. A couple nearing retirement, Mr. and Mrs. Ed Lievens, who had neither met Father Cassedy nor heard of him, read the article. Based on that one story, they made a decision to give their 960-acre ranch to Cassedy for his boys' ranch (North Dakotan, 1951).

Group facilities for dependent children were almost nonexistent in North Dakota in 1949. With the exception of St. John's Orphanage and the Children's Home Society Orphanage (now The Village Family Services) in Fargo, and the Nellie Svee Home in Devils Lake (now Lutheran Social Services), there were no private congregate facilities in the state for dependent children. Some children were inappropriately placed at the State

Hospital or the State Training School; others were simply left to find their own way. Home on the Range for Boys was to meet the needs of delinquent youth who, for a variety of reasons, were deprived of a suitable home life but whose behavior did not require treatment or incarceration, only nurturance and direction.

Cassedy, an Irish priest with a New Jersey accent, established the home near Sentinel Butte in the spring of 1950. The first three boys accepted at the ranch were welcomed into a 32- x 48-ft remodeled granary. The facility was started with little money, and a statement by the bishop, "You're on your own" (Raymond, 1962). There were many problems facing Father Cassedy. Although the buildings were good, they were not adequate for a boys' home. Father Cassedy, who grew up in Jersey City, N.J., knew nothing about farming. The ranch had no poultry or livestock to provide food for the residents. Livestock was needed if the ranch were to be even partially self-supporting.

Many imaginative and successful fund raisers were held across the nation to benefit Home on the Range for Boys. The Eagles organization nationwide adopted the cause of the ranch and became their single-most-ardent supporter.

"Father Cassedy had the ranch going before I got there," said Fahnlander, "but they were living hand-to-mouth. There were 28 kids there, all jammed into what we now call the administration building. There were 12 to a room with a bed for each, but they all had to share one chest of drawers and one steel locker."

Money was tight and the cause was a noble one. People wanted to help. Two such supporters who came forward were brothers Jim and Tom Tescher. Parishioners of Father Fahnlander's, they came to him in 1956 with the idea of a star-studded rodeo to benefit the ranch.

Discussing the rodeo, Champions Ride Match, which was for years North Dakota's largest athletic event, Father Bill said, "Most of the credit goes to Jim and Tom. The Schnells had their Match of Champions bronc riding in Dickinson each August and got a good draw at it. Jim and Tom said, 'Why don't we do the same thing here?' Ray Schnell, a board member and owner of Schnells' Livestock Auction Market, Dickinson, got the crew of guys to build the arena. Jim and Tom invited their friends to participate."

Debuting in May 1957, it was cold, damp, and windy when the first horse bucked in the freshly worked dirt. "It was a miserable, awful, horrible day," remembered Father Bill. "These cowboys were so cold they wore big mackinaws and built a fire behind the chutes with the leftover scraps of wood from the arena!" Spectators parked their cars around the perimeter of the newly constructed arena, content to watch from the comfort of their vehicles.

Father Fahnlander, a city boy, had only been to a couple of rodeos in Dickinson by the time he was hosting one of his own at the ranch. A rookie to the sport, he was suddenly brushing shoulders with the likes of Casey Tibbs and Bill Lindermann, who came the first year (Champions Ride Rodeo Program, 1984).

"The first couple of years the cowboys didn't take any pay checks. Later we added prize money because that was their livelihood and you couldn't expect them to never make any money coming to our rodeo. I spent time at Denver and other rodeos, hanging around behind the chutes, getting to know these guys. I'd watch and see who was doing good and ask them to our rodeo. I saw Larry Mahan ride in Denver in January when he was just getting started. I liked him, thought he was good, so I invited him to Champions Ride."

Recounting Mahan's first appearance, Father Bill noted "he went on a hot streak and led the all-around (by the time he got to Sentinel Butte in August) and turned out to be a drawing card." Mahan would go on to be a six-time professional world champion all-around cowboy.

Then, as now, the rodeo was billed as family entertainment for a family cause. Champions Ride scored big from the very beginning: cowboys found top quality stock on which to compete and win prize money; families enjoyed an afternoon of quality entertainment in the colorful Bad Lands; Home On The Range residents benefitted from the proceeds and experience of producing the rodeo.

Since 1961 the invitational rodeo has been held the first Sunday in August. Through the years some events, such as calf roping and barrel racing, have been added or dropped, but saddle bronc riding has always remained the feature. Each bronc rider is assured of at least two rides astride topnotch stock. The six leading scorers compete in the saddle bronc finals featuring pro rodeo's most respected horses. Champions Ride, one of the nation's few remaining saddle bronc matches, has been called a preview of the National Finals Rodeo (NFR). Many of the horses and cowboys participating at Home On The Range will appear at the NFR. Father Fahnlander had his own depiction, "Our saddle bronc riding is like the Major League All-Star Game."

"The best ride I ever saw was Tom Tescher riding Trails End," said Father Bill. "He doffed his hat when he got off... and had a grin like his throat was slit." The bronc, from the Oral Zumwalt Rodeo Company, Missoula, Mont., was a spoiled pack horse. Tescher's name went into the history books that year – 1960 – for marking the highest score at Champions Ride. Zumwalt's bronc was voted outstanding bucking horse, garnering a trophy for his owner.

"I'm a drugstore cowboy," admitted Father Bill, and for the most part he steered clear of horses. So, he wasn't too excited about Ray Schnell's idea that Father Fahnlander ride horseback in the grand entry one year, along with the rodeo contestants as they were introduced. Father Bill's first choice of a mount was a pinto pony. Schnell vetoed that, suggesting instead a big, athletic horse belonging to cowboy Dean Oliver. Oliver, a calf roper, was built about as differently from Father Bill as possible. A full head or more taller than the priest, Oliver's legs were much longer than Fahnlander's.

"I couldn't reach the stirrups," recalled Father Bill, explaining what happened once he was mounted. Riding a horse trained to sprint after a fast-moving calf, seated on a borrowed saddle, he came blasting into the arena. "I held onto the saddle horn, held on for all I was worth and pulled leather all the way around the arena." As soon as he touched the reins, meaning only to slow the horse, the highly-trained animal put on the brakes, skidding to a complete stop. The priest-turned-cowboy catapulted forward, stopped mercifully by his arms clinging around the animal's neck.

Father Fahnlander termed that ride as "possibly the most embarrassing moment in my life." Addressing the crowd shortly afterwards, he told the assembled rodeo fans, "Well, we've already had our clown act!" That would be the last time Father Bill participated on horseback in a rodeo grand entry. (Champions Ride Rodeo Program, 1984), (Cowboy Chronicle, 2001).

Receipts from fund raisers like the rodeo, and outright donations of food and money, made it possible for Father Cassedy to pay the bills. In the early years the boys came from North Dakota, California, Illinois, and a half-dozen other states from across the Midwest. Most of the boys were products of broken homes, abandoned either through divorce or the death of parents (Mulhall, 1953). Whatever their background, placement at the ranch was voluntary. It was not unusual for a boy to stay at the ranch for several years, leaving only after graduation from high school, or when he turned 18.

A regimented routine applied to all boys. Those who milked the cows arose at 5:00 a.m., and they, in turn, awakened the others at 6:30. After religious services and breakfast, each boy was to clean his room and do his chores. The boys attended school in Sentinel Butte, and later in nearby Beach when the Sentinel Butte School closed. (For a short time, the 7th and 8th grade students were taught in the library within Eagle Hall.) After dinner was served at 6:00 p.m., the boys amused themselves in the recreation room or out-of-doors until lights out. On non-school days they did ranch work; on holidays and Sundays they played host to visitors. Nonsectarian in admissions, boys were required to attend a church of their choice. Catholic Mass was held each morning for those who wished to attend (Barker, 1954).

Letters poured in, imploring Father Cassedy to take far more boys than he had room or resources to accommodate. The stress on this man, who had a heart condition, was intense. "Father Cassedy was afraid of the outcome of his ranch," said Fahnlander. "Materially, the place didn't stand a chance! But, Cassedy would go back to Jersey City to raise funds. I'd stay at the Ranch and run things and Father Cassedy would be gone for two months at a time, off on fund-raising trips. More times than not, there would be bills stacked on his desk and nothing to pay them with. He always told me the money would come. I learned to trust in the Lord through Father Cassedy."

"I never laid awake worrying about finances although we were just barely living hand to mouth," admitted Fahnlander in a January 2000 interview with Marge Grosz, editor of the Dakota Catholic Action, official publication of the Bismarck Diocese. "I always believed the Lord was taking care of us and I still believe that." He admitted that his biggest problem was that he always had more to do than he could ever possibly hope to accomplish.

Family members were summoned to Father Cassedy's bedside in October 1957. Stricken by a heart attack, the priest lay in critical condition. "Doc" Bush, Beach's country doctor, insisted Cassedy take time off to recover. Bush took care of Cassedy at his lodge in Beach after the attack. The slight-built priest then spent two years in Jersey in a nursing home.

Father Fahnlander recounts the series of events: "After I had been at Sentinel Butte for about four years, Father Cassedy suffered a severe heart attack. His coming back was doubtful. I was reluctant to accept the assignment to become his successor.

"I went to Minot to visit Monsignor Hogan. His prolonged cancer illness had brought him to the point of dying. As I had done for all the years I had known him, I laid my problem on him, pacing the floor beside his bed. I

Monsignor John W. Hogan, who so greatly
influenced Bill Fahnlander, not only as a child, but
as a young priest. Father Fahnlander kept this framed
photo on the top of the dresser in his bedroom.
(Photo courtesy of Fahnlander Family.)

told him, 'The bishop wants me to take the job at Home on the Range. No one else seems to want it, and the kids are starting to get to me.' In his weakened condition, he spoke with real effort, 'The only thing that counts is the will of God.'

"I left him and pondered his words. A week later at his funeral, in February 1959, I told the bishop I was ready to accept the assignment at Home on the Range. Years later, I can still hear those words as if it were yesterday. This was the greatest lesson in faith that I've ever had" (St. Leo's: The First 100 Years, 1986).

Father Fahnlander assumed the role of interim superintendent, relinquishing his parish responsibilities and taking up residence at the boys' ranch in March 1959. "Strangely, I succeeded Father Cassedy at St. Mary's in Bismarck when I was first ordained," said Fahnlander, "and then I succeeded him at Sentinel Butte" (Dakota Catholic Action, 2000).

In a letter dated July 27, 1959, Father Fahnlander wrote to Father Cassedy, bringing him up-to-date on happenings at the Ranch while he was recovering…

> Dear Elwood:
>
> During the latter part of June, at the suggestion of Phil Bigley and Bob Hansen, I made four different state conventions – the Bi-State of North and South Dakota at Devils Lake, the Indiana at South Bend, the Minnesota at East Grand Forks, and the Wisconsin at Kenosha. As long as I was doing this, I managed to get to a two-day annual meeting of the National Association of Homes for Boys. I thought I might learn something, but found that I learned most of all that this is the best place of them all. All of them had worse problems than we have, and what is more, I don't think any of them are doing a better job with the kids than we are getting done… and without the help of the "professional" help they have…
>
> I am running out now. It has been two days since I began this letter, and it seems that every time I get going well, one of the kids comes in for something. Better I should get it off before anything else comes up, you might not get it until Christmas.

Champions Ride Rodeo, May 1959, served as ground-breaking ceremony for Eagle Hall. Joining in the festivities that day were movie and singing star Rex Allen and his band. Father Fahnlander (second from the right) squeezed in to make it a quartet, at least for the afternoon.
(Photo from archives of Home On The Range.)

Following four years of "Give a Buck for a Brick" fund raising by the Eagles, ground-breaking ceremonies were held in May of 1959 for a long-awaited gymnasium. The event was held in conjunction with the Champions Ride Match Rodeo. Cowboy singer and movie star Rex Allen donated his time for a special concert performance that day – in the rodeo arena. The $200,000 complex – a combination gym, chapel, library-study hall, recreation room, and dormitory was appropriately named Eagle Hall.

By 1959, the census at the ranch had increased to nearly 40 boys. Father Cassedy felt well enough to return to the ranch in October and penned his annual Christmas letter. "Doc Bush told me he wouldn't last if he came back," said Father Fahnlander. "Father Cassedy was frail, but he wanted to try it. Doc Bush would only let him work half-days, and even at that he only lasted two weeks." On October 15, 1959, at the age of 51, Father Cassedy died. "I was with him when he had his last heart attack," said Fahnlander, "he lived for a couple days afterwards."

Following funeral services in Beach, Father Cassedy was laid to rest as he requested, on a hill that overlooks the ranch. His grave is marked by a simple, unobtrusive marble-encased monument. Engraved on the capping stone is a brief summary of his life (Christensen, 1963). Father Fahnlander, the interim assistant, became Father Fahnlander, the permanent successor.

"Father Cassedy had a lot of foresight," related Fahnlander. "I respected him more in his death than in his life, once I started filling his shoes. I thought the FOE (Eagles) would drop me and Home On The Range after Cassedy's death. I thought they were doing it for him. They couldn't have treated me better if I'd been the King of Siam! I found their interest was in the kids, not just Father Cassedy.

"The Eagles call themselves 'People Helping People,' and they live that motto," emphasized Fahnlander. "There's a long list of charities they support. They've been marvelous to us. They built Eagle Hall for us. They're not just purely social. I like to add to their motto and say they're 'People Having Fun Helping People.'

"The Eagles Auxiliaries used to adopt the boys and remember 'em at Christmas, Valentine's Day and on their birthdays... In Cleveland, Ohio, one time (at the Grand Aerie Convention), a group's boy had just left the ranch and it was needing another one. Well, someone noticed I had a hole in the sole of my boots. They adopted me instead of a boy. Ever since, all the Auxiliaries – they've put out a big act for me."

The May 2001 issue of *Eagle Magazine* described the scene when the Auxiliaries put on their "big act" for him: "He would submit with typical good-humor and that warm smile to another skit performed by his adopted "moms," the Past Grand Madam Presidents, whom he loved and whose hijinks he tolerated as graciously as any son put into the spotlight by proud and fawning parents." On hand to greet his countless Eagle friends and express his eternal gratitude for their continuing support of Home On The Range, Father Bill attended more than 40 International Grand Aerie Conventions across the United States and Canada. One person described Father Fahnlander's welcome as being equal to that given a Hollywood celebrity. In their minds, he was a star in his own right.

Fahnlander also credited the Knights of Columbus for being great fund raisers, especially with their Shamrock Sales each year. Catholic Daughters helped over the years with potlucks, and their members faithfully made a quilt for every child at the ranch (Dakota Catholic Action, 2000).

Still, it was tough stepping up to the plate and taking over for the ranch's celebrated founder. When asked by Dorgan as to how many hats he wore and what his job description was, Father Bill related this typically delightful Fahnlander story: "One time when I was delivering clothes for my mom, I carried a bunch of dresses on hangers into this place. The lady inside was pounding a nail into the wall. I said, 'So, you're a carpenter too!' She replied, 'Yeah, hell, I'm *everything*!' I remembered her many times while I was at Home On The Range, like when I was unplugging a toilet. I could say the same thing. I was everything! I learned a lot of things they don't teach you in the seminary."

A letter dated October 21, 1959, addressed to Mr. L. N. Morrisson, Ann Arbor, Mich., captured Father Bill's candid emotions when faced with the reality of his situation:

> Dear "Sarge":
> We (Cassedy and Fahnlander) had eagerly anticipated working togther – I was to take the responsibility of running things here, and he planned to go "on the road," and we felt that this would work out beautifully to make Home on the Range for Boys better than ever.
> God apparently had other plans, and called him to his reward before his time. It would be a lie if I were to say that

I understand just why. I do realize, though, that God's wisdom will prove itself in time, and that with God's help, Home on the Range will go on. It may be that from his place in heaven that Father Cassedy can do more than he could do here.

I am well aware that I can never really take his place here. All I can say is that I will do my best. I do hope that you will slip in a little prayer for me now and then that I will be given the direction and strength to do a good job. It was most consoling to read your letter and read of your assured support in the future. I know I will need it more than ever...

I had looked forward to living my life out here at Home on the Range, but the thought of being without Father Cassedy had not entered my mind. Now I am plumb scared at the prospect of having the entire responsibility. For two years, since Father Cassedy's heart attack, I have pretty much been running things here. I had looked forward to him being back and that we would take care of things together. Having had this experience, I know what a responsibility faces me...

One short year later, it was time for the traditional Christmas letter to be written and mailed. Father Cassedy had penned the correspondence from 1951 until 1959. In the fall of 1960, the task fell to Father Fahnlander:

It will soon be Christmas, and I know that you are accustomed to receiving Father Cassedy's letter at this time of year. Since his untimely death a little over one year ago, I have been carrying on this work he began. While the boys and I miss him terribly, I do want you to know that the Home on the Range for Boys is continuing.

Ten years have passed since Father Cassedy moved out here with three boys. Many boys have found a home here in these years. They are scattered all over the United States, where they are making us very proud of them. Yes, much progress has been made in those 10 years.

In this year we completed a new building, Eagle Hall.

Along with room for almost twice as many boys, it contains a gym, library, recreation room, and chapel. This beautiful building was made possible through the gifts of our special friends, the Fraternal Order of Eagles. Our family has now grown from the original three boys to almost 40 boys.

You, our friends, are responsible for this progress. You have been interested and generous. You have always responded to our needs with your material and moral support. Because of you, first Father Cassedy, and now I can maintain this home for boys – boys who have had little chance in life until they came here – now these boys have the chance to develop into useful, God-fearing citizens.

Father Bill became quite proficient at letter writing. Perhaps he gleaned the skill from Father Hogan back at St. Leo's. He was as eloquent on paper as he was in person. And, his knack for handling an interview – radio, television, newspaper, or magazine – made it look effortless. Father Fahnlander's days were filled with both. Sometimes he even authored magazine articles himself, all the while balancing a hectic travel and speaking schedule, supervising staff, spending time with the boys, and keeping in touch with his family.

With more than 40 boys in residence, Father Fahnlander found it necessary to increase both income and work opportunities. Caged layers were added to the farm program in 1961. Eventually, they would produce over four thousand eggs daily for use at the ranch, as well as for sale to retail customers in Beach and Dickinson, N. Dak, and Spokane, Wash.

Father Fahnlander began making plans for a building in which the boys could learn carpentry, auto mechanics, welding, and sheet metal. It would be known as the Schnell Building in honor of director Ray Schnell. A meat processing and freezer plant was built by the Eagles of Michigan so that slaughtering and processing could be done on-site – and at the same time teach some boys to be meat cutters. Grain harvesting was still done the old-fashioned way, with binders and a threshing machine; straw and hay bales were stacked by hand. Father Fahnlander defended the method, saying it helps all the boys to be involved. Though it meant going into debt, a quarter of tillable land was purchased, bringing the ranch holdings to a total of 1120 acres. This enabled the ranch to raise more feed and enlarge the beef

Father Richard Connolly (left) and Father Bill flank comedian
Frank Fontaine at the 1979 Fraternal Order of Eagles International
Convention in Kansas City, Missouri. Fontaine, himself an Eagle
member and delegate to the convention, is best remembered for his
Crazy Guggenheim character on the popular 1960's Jackie Gleason Show.
(Photo from Home On The Range archives.)

and dairy herds. These projects all took money.

In addition to administering the facility, Father Fahnlander was the chief fund raiser. He explained his methodology in a 1963 Christmas message to Eagle Auxiliary members:

> Before I accepted this work, I dreaded the thought of begging for help to carry on the work that Father Cassedy began. I suppose I felt too proud to beg. Now that I have been here for several years, I don't recall that I ever have had to "beg" for anything... Instead, people have asked "What can we give?" or "What do you need?" Their basic love for their fellow men has overwhelmed me...

Boastful when it came to the accomplishments of his boys, Father Fahnlander routinely minimized his role at Home on the Range for Boys. Besides an insurmountable work load of day-to-day administrative duties and time spent with the boys, Father Bill was also in great demand as a banquet and convention speaker. If it meant he might be able to spread the word about the ranch and generate contributions to sustain it, he would address a group almost anywhere.

He made an annual pilgrimage to visit with his Eagle friends at the International Convention of the Grand Aerie. In Minneapolis he and several boys met former President Truman. Other notables who came to know of the Ranch through personal contact with Father Fahnlander included Danny Thomas, Paul Harvey, Bob Hope, and Dr. Karl Menninger.

Ten thousand Eagles were in Miami when he had a chance to rub shoulders with several former athletes: boxers Gene Fullmer and Tony "Two Ton" Galento; along with two of Notre Dame's Four Horsemen, Don Miller and Jim Crowley. Fullmer, who reigned as middleweight champion from 1957 until 1962, was inducted into the Boxing Hall of Fame in 1974. Heavyweight boxer Galento fought Joe Louis in 1939, losing in a fourth-round TKO. Louis often said later that Galento was one of the toughest, if not the toughest man, he ever fought. Galento went on to have an impressive movie career, appearing in or contributing to four movies, including On the Waterfront.

A reporter noted that Father Bill, "a slight, wiry, mild-mannered man, seemed out of place in the plush room next to the athletes." That was until

Delegates and guests at the 1968 FOE Convention
included Father Fahnlander, Past Iowa State President Charles Kacer,
and former heavy-weight boxer Tony Galento. Galento, who was
called one of the toughest men ever to enter the ring, went on to
build a second career starring in Hollywood movies.
(From the archives of the Fraternal Order of Eagles.)

Father Fahnlander told them that he, too, was once an athlete – on two state championship high school basketball teams in Minot. But always his favorite story was about how the ranch came into being (Holmberg, 1976).

The following letters and articles from Father Fahnlander's first decade at Home on the Range for Boys provide a vivid glimpse into his daily life and that of the boys living at the ranch:

Fall of 1961, Home on the Range for Boys Christmas letter:

We have been able to undertake a new project – caged layers. With this we are supplying the surrounding communities (and ourselves) with eggs. Together with the beef and dairy cattle, we can produce much of our own food, and some income. As my family grows, the chickens give another project to keep the boys busy.

Over 40 boys have joined our family. They range in age from twelve to eighteen years. The high school boys attend the public school in Beach, N. Dak. For the second straight year, one of my boys was elected captain of the football team. In three of the past four years one of my boys has been elected 'King of the Prom' by the students in school. This gives you an idea of how well my boys are accepted by their fellow students.

I hope you don't mind my 'doting' over my boys a little. I am very proud of them. At the same time, I can't help but wonder what they might have become without this chance. You and many other good people have made this home possible. First, you helped Father Cassedy to found Home on the Range and then to build and maintain it. Since his death, you have helped me to carry on the work he began…"

Bismarck Tribune article, by Bob Raymond, October 19, 1962:

"Three Years After His Death Memory of Father Cassedy Still Vivid at Home On The Range"

Some of the boys hitchhike in. Others come from the seamy slums of major cities. They all arrive voluntarily. And

The ranch hands living at Home on the Range for Boys
gather in the newly completed Eagle Hall for this 1961 family photo.
Father Fahnlander flashes his familiar smile after successfully getting
all his boys groomed, dressed, and in position for the camera.
(Photo from Home On The Range archives.)

after departing, many seek to return.

The desire to come back is just one of the many wonderful attributes of the Home on the Range for Boys at Sentinel Butte, this month celebrating its 12th anniversary, and...

Paying solemn tribute to its founder, The Rev. Elwood E. Cassedy, who died three years ago this week after literally working his heart out for "my boys."

It is guided by the work-hardened but gentle hand of the Rev. William J. Fahnlander, Father Cassedy's assistant and successor, who accepted the task with more than apprehension, but now wouldn't leave for all the treasures of China.

"I wanted to be pastor of a church," the greying, young Minot-born priest says. "I enjoyed working with youngsters, but I must admit, the thought of being another cowboy priest leading a flock of youth in the wilderness was not my strongest desire... Today I can conceive of no more fulfilling position on earth... "

Minot Daily News article, Saturday, July 6, 1963:

"Home On The Range Testimonial To Priest's Faith In Boys"

To help maintain the home, Father Fahnlander directs the activities of four counselors, a practical nurse, a combination cook-laundress and barber, a ranch hand and a stenographer.

The volume of Father Fahnlander's mail, phone calls and such queries from the boys as, "Father, may I see you a minute," is almost staggering. Yet no request for help or information is ever denied by the slight, soft-spoken former parish priest...

One former Home on the Range boy, Father Fahnlander said, is working toward his Ph.D. in physical chemistry; several others are upperclass college students and quite a few are in the armed services...

Some of the staff, like Matilda Decker, have been here almost from the beginning of the home. Many of the counselors are seminarians, working at the home during the summer months to gain required practical experience before being ordained into the priesthood.

"We've received requests from seminarians all over the nation to come to the ranch for a summer," Father Fahnlander said...

Each boy is assigned a specific task for which, if practical, he volunteers. For their work, they receive an allowance from which they are expected to buy all their clothing and incidentals.

Their chores can range from managing the chicken house where some 3,900 eggs are received, checked, washed and crated daily, to the more mundane tasks, such as maintaining "mud alley," the foyer to Eagle Hall where the boys are required to take off their shoes and hang up their wraps before entering the sleeping sections of the building.

"It's amazing to see how some of these boys – many from the streets of big cities like Chicago and New York – have taken to the openness of the prairies and to tasks like cutting hay, picking eggs and milking cows," Father Fahnlander said.

The Minot Eagle article, April 1964:
"Dakota Aerie Notes," by Father Fahnlander

With two good crop years behind us, we have been in good shape for feed for the livestock. I really think that we could get by for another two years with the supply we have on hand. This means that the livestock will eat well, and when they eat well, we eat well, too.

My family has grown to forty-eight boys, the largest number we have ever had. I might add, it is the maximum number we expect to have from now on. Father Cassedy was in favor of keeping Home on the Range small, and I heartily agree with this thinking. This way we can keep the family atmosphere. The group here now represents twelve different states, seven religious faiths, and four racial groups. In spite of their varied backgrounds, each boy has one thing in common with the others – he is a boy who needed a chance. This brings them together into a closely knit group.

With 5000 caged laying hens we have a chance to eat eggs for breakfast once in a while. When some of the hens get lazy, we eat chicken. Handling a flock of hens this size, and processing their eggs, has proved to be an excellent work project that keeps a good-sized crew of boys busy.

In less than 15 years since Father Cassedy first brought three boys out here, over 250 boys have found a home here for periods ranging from a few months to nine years. Many of the former boys have been back to visit these past few months. During the Christmas holidays three were back from great distances. One came from California, one from Iowa and one from Nevada. It is always good to see them come back and hear them tell how much living here has meant to them. It is even better to see that they have become fine young men who are now an asset to society…

With this many boys I can hardly say that "All is Quiet on the Western Front," but at least we are still in there pitching…

Fall of 1964, Home on the Range for Boys Christmas letter:

As Christmas and the end of another year approaches, this is a good opportunity to thank you for your kindness to us and let you know how things are going here at Home on the Range.

The past year has brought us the blessings of another good crop of hay, feed grains, and corn for silage. Our family grew to 48 boys this year. Yet I still find it necessary to turn many boys away. Hardly a day passes without at least one telephone call, letter, or telegram asking me to take a boy. To say, "Sorry we have no more room," is the difficult part of my work.

Along with our blessings we had our problems. Last spring, shortly after the Alaskan earthquake, our well went dry. We had to drill a new well – and had to go down 1510 feet to get an adequate supply of water. This cost over $9,000 – quite an unexpected blow to our budget. Fortunately, we were able to drill on credit…

Fall of 1969, Home on the Range for Boys Christmas letter:

God has been good to us. We had a wonderful hay crop, and the small grain and corn crops were very good. Putting up hay kept a crew of boys busy in the earlier part of the summer, and at harvest time the whole crew worked like beavers shocking grain and later threshing the grain. Cutting the grain with binders, shocking, and threshing are the "old-fashioned" way to harvest, but it helps all 48 boys to get into the act.

Six boys graduated from high school last spring. Two are now in college, one is in the Navy, and three have jobs. Many of the nearly 400 former boys who have lived here have been back "home" to visit. Some came with their wives and families. We are proud of these many fine young men who still regard Home on the Range as "home." We all think of them as part of our "family" here.

With the completion of the new Interstate-94 Highway, we are within sight of the road. If you travel in this direction, we hope you will stop to see us…

The 1970s were a time of change and continued growth. July 1972 saw the dedication of a new, modern dairy barn, designed to house 110 dairy cows. Two thousand people attended the festivities. Father Fahnlander frequently made mention of "his boys" stopping back to visit. If they could not visit in person, they called or wrote, often including a few dollars to help the cause. Father Bill found great joy in their visits and wrote lengthy replies to their letters. The doting father was shining from within when he wrote, "It means so much to have them come back and talk about the good times – and even more when we see them as well-adjusted young men."

Times were changing, nonetheless. The needs of youth referred to the ranch were becoming increasingly more complicated and required additional services. The first social worker hired at Home On The Range came on staff in May 1975. Two more would be hired by the end of the decade. Chemical dependency was becoming more prevalent in the boys accepted at the ranch.

Fall of 1975, Home on the Range for Boys Christmas letter:

In early July we had a joyous celebration commemorating our twenty-fifth anniversary since Father Cassedy founded our ranch home. A reunion of former boys with their wives and families proved to be a truly rewarding experience, I have never seen a group have more good, clean fun than these young men with their families had when they got together here.

Since there was this span of years between them, many had never met each other before. However, the bond of being part of the Home on the Range "family" proved to be enough to make them all feel close to one another. My conviction that this work is really worthwhile was deepened more than ever after seeing young men from all over the country back home to renew old friendships and make new friends…

Fall of 1977, Home on the Range for Boys Christmas letter:

Our year has been one of mixed blessings and setbacks, which is really the story of life for most everyone…

Our household of over forty boys has managed to keep busy with school and chores around the ranch. These chores vary from milking over 80 cows, working in our auto, welding and wood shop, keeping up the yards, helping in the kitchen, to housecleaning. We try to rotate them around so they get a taste of various kinds of work.

It was a dry summer, so our feed supply for our cattle is in short supply, otherwise we would be milking more cows. We did manage to hustle up feed through the kindness of farmers and ranchers in our territory, so we hope to make it through the winter…

In late September we had the misfortune of having one of our barns burn down. The fire began right near the hay and straw which were stored there, so it really got out of control in a hurry. This, of course, was a real loss, and even more so, with the loss of thirteen calves and three cows…

CHAPTER THREE

Made Holy by Faith

Father Fahnlander celebrated both his 60th birthday and marked 24 years of service to Home On The Range in 1981. Programs, emphasizing treatment and prevention, were designed to guide a boy's behavior before he became enmeshed in serious trouble. Twenty-six full-time staff were employed: 14 to work directly with the boys as counselors and case workers. The success rate was calculated at approximately 90 percent. Those successfully discharged returned to their homes or went on to school. Most of those who did not make it at the ranch were committed to the State Industrial School or a similar institution (Anderson, 1983).

With Father Fahnlander nearing retirement, Mohall, N. Dak. native Winston E. Satran was appointed director in 1986. The dormitories were filled to capacity with 52 boys from North Dakota, Montana, California, and Nevada. Satran's prior experience included work as a counselor at Dakota Boys Ranch, seven years as deputy warden of the North Dakota State Penitentiary and seven years as warden. Father Bill's retirement as superintendent was to be effective December 31, 1987. Though retired, he would remain on the board of directors, serve as chaplain, and hold the title of "superintendent emeritus."

Fall 1987, Father Fahnlander's farewell Christmas letter:

As Christmas and the end of the year nears, you good friends of Home On The Range come to mind. I have experienced your friendship for 32 years now. As I look back over those years, two wonderful experiences stand out in my mind. First is the joy and satisfaction that comes when a former boy, who is now a successful citizen, comes back to visit and expresses thanks, and the second is the heartwarming experience of having such caring friends like you, who have done so much to make Home On The Range what it is today.

Father Fahnlander models a new vestment,
a gift from his "adopted" Eagle moms. Posing in front of the
altar at the Church of St. John the Baptist, Beach,
the gift was given on the occasion of his retirement as
Home On The Range Superintendent.
(Photo courtesy of Lois Nelson; donated to Home On The Range archives.)

Just 30 years ago this past month, Father Cassedy, our founder, suffered a severe heart attack which left him unable to continue as our superintendent. Since that time, I have been in the position of carrying on the work he began. The years have been fulfilling with countless occurrences of wonderful satisfaction, and times of trial and anxiety mixed between. I know I would never trade these years for all the wealth in the world.

For over a year now, Winston Satran has been our director. I feel he has proven himself as a most capable and dedicated person in this role. With him in the position, I now feel the time has come when I can, with a feeling of absolute confidence in his ability to carry on this work, step down and hand the reins over to him. My age and physical condition is such that I feel the need to slow the pace of my activity. With all this in mind, our board of directors has agreed to allow me to retire as superintendent at the end of the year.

I will continue to function as the chaplain and continue to serve on our board of directors. In that way, I will be able to still be involved with Home On The Range without the administrative responsibilities.

At this time I want to express my heartfelt thanks to you, our friends, Winston Satran, the present staff and all who have served on our staff throughout the years, for making these 32 years of time a satisfaction and joy. Lastly, I am grateful to all our boys, those here now and former boys whose lives have been touched by Home On The Range, and have responded to that touch. May God bless all of you.

With those five paragraphs, Father Fahnlander symbolically cleared out his desk at Home On The Range. He never disengaged himself completely from the ranch, but was freed from the day-to-day concerns of managing the small community known by locals as "The Ranch." He assumed the role of chaplain at Home On The Range and continued with parish duties in Beach and Sentinel Butte.

On July 1, 1991, Father Fahnlander retired from his assignment at Beach and Sentinel Butte. He moved to Mandan, N. Dak., taking up the position of priest in residence at the Church of Christ the King. Another blest parish came to know the counsel of Father Bill, and his circle of friends broadened once again.

In 1996 he retired from Christ the King and relocated to Emmaus Place, a retirement home for priests, if it could even be called retirement. Surviving a near-fatal abdominal aneurysm in May 1996, Fahnlander came back stronger and more active than he had been in years, his calendar brimming with dates to fill in for priests throughout the diocese. Acquaintances encouraged him to slow down, but over and over he assured them that he was feeling better than he ever had.

Father Bill reveled in something he'd not known for years: free time. He enjoyed few things more than an outing to one of North Dakota's casinos. A trip to Minnesota to visit his sister Eloise, niece Mary Jo, and nephew Bill, necessitated a "blessing" of the casinos in the Land of 10,000 Lakes. In fact, a pilgrimage just about anywhere could lead past a casino, if Father Bill was planning the route. And he frequently came home with a big jackpot – promptly allocating it among his favorite charities. There were those who accused Father Fahnlander of having an unfair advantage when he hit the casinos. Perhaps it was because the Pit Boss in the Sky knew his booty would be so willingly shared with others.

Major transformations in programming were to occur in the next decade as the ranch responded to changing needs. In August 1990, after 40 years of serving only boys, the doors were opened to female residents. The change reflected the lack of adequate facilities for girls and was in response to a recommendation from state child welfare officials in North Dakota. To accommodate the change in population, the official name, Home on the Range for Boys, was shortened to Home On The Range. Licensing now permitted 79 residents at the Sentinel Butte Ranch: 20 girls, 57 boys, and 2 emergency shelter care beds for boys. Although residents formerly came from states throughout the union, by 1990 only three states were represented: Montana, North Dakota, and Minnesota.

As North Dakota had done just a few years earlier, Montana requested that Home On The Range expand services for girls in eastern Montana. By the end of 1993, a four-bedroom home on 65 acres, six miles north of Glendive, was ready for occupancy. Home On The Range – Big Sky Ranch was licensed as a moderate-level therapeutic group home, serving eight girls.

Experience gained at Big Sky Ranch proved invaluable when Home On The Range was asked to expand services in the Fargo area. Licensed to care for 12 chemically dependent adolescent males between the ages of 10 and 18, Victory Ranch was designed to serve youth who had received initial treatment for addiction, but required a reinforcing step prior to returning to their home community. A 12½-acre parcel of land near Hector Field in north Fargo was purchased for the home. The first resident was accepted in March 1997.

A special year of celebration at Home On The Range was declared in 1996, to recognize several personal and professional milestones in Father Fahnlander's life: his 75th birthday in February; the 50th Jubilee of his ordination as a priest; and in August, the 40th anniversary of the Champions Ride Match Rodeo. The rodeo begun by Father Bill back in 1957 had become a nationally known event. Staff took up a collection and made arrangements for an all-expense-paid trip for Fahnlander to attend the National Finals Rodeo (NFR) in Las Vegas. During his years as superintendent, he had never been able to get away to attend the NFR, an event he had always hoped to attend.

When Father Bill retired from Home On The Range, he left behind an amazing collection of plaques and trophies, honors bestowed upon him since his earliest days as superintendent. There were more than any home or office could possibly accommodate, let alone a man who would soon be moving into retirement quarters. Among the many are four awards which represent Father Fahnlander's wide range of benefaction.

In August 1980, the International Grand Auxiliary, Fraternal Order of Eagles, selected Father Fahnlander as their Man of the Year. Only seven such awards have been given by the Grand Auxiliary in their 76-year history: two to United States Congressmen, two to Past Grand Aerie officers, one to M. Daniel Splain III who served as secretary to the Grand Board of Trustees and Grand Tribunal, and one each to Father John Connelly, and Father Fahnlander. The official proceedings of the convention recorded the festivities:

Toast mistress Chloe Honeycutt, addressing the women's assembly during a banquet, said, "You can't be an Eagle, very long at least, without hearing about Home On The Range. Our guest has been a Big Brother, a Father, Mother, Buddy. You name it – for many, many years to 50 boys at one time... He is also a Brother Eagle... Sisters, please welcome Father Fahnlander, Home on the Range for Boys. Father."

Unable to let such a perfect introduction pass without capitalizing on it, Father Bill was quick to lay his first witticism on the crowd after acknowledging the delegates and guests:

> You know, I am trying to figure this one out. You were talking about what I was to those boys. Okay, I am here as a Brother. You are my Sisters, and down there are some of my Moms, and I am a Father. I am not sure if I might not be my own grandfather or something...
>
> When I learned that I was to be your speaker at this banquet, and I heard that Bill Cosby was going to be here, I prayed that I would be on before him. And I watched the door faithfully. I thought, I am going to make it – and then he showed up.
>
> I have just come from Home On The Range in western North Dakota. We are experiencing a real drought there. Since a year ago in May, we have had less than three inches of rain. If you want to know how really dry it is, well there is a little lake near us. Recently we took a water sample out of that and had it tested. The water showed 23 percent moisture. Last week when we milked the cows, we got powdered milk.
>
> When I was flying out here there was some turbulence and the plane was really bouncing something terrible. The lady sitting next to me, she said, 'Can't you do something to stop that?' I said, 'Sorry lady, I am in sales, not in management.

As conventioneers had come to expect, Father Fahnlander played the consummate comedian, delivering one joke after another story, after another one-liner. Laughter filled the great hall. Then it was time to get serious and deliver the message Cincinnati convention goers were expecting. Only, he couldn't get too serious, instead, slipping in that famous humor as he went along. It was difficult to tell if he was spicing up his jokes with success stories about boys who had lived at the ranch or telling stories about the ranch intermingled with mischief. Either way, the audience loved it. Indications of laughter are scattered throughout the recorded text of his speech.

Referring to a recent 30th anniversary reunion of former boys, Father Bill got somewhat more serious and started talking about the boys:

> One was back and I had lunch with him, and you know it was so delightful. They had a boy in the fifth grade and a boy in the seventh grade. When we finished eating, not a word was said. The little kid picked up the dishes and took them out to the kitchen. This was a boy who wasn't able to finish high school... He is working for a large printing company. He has been working with them for 14 years. He is a foreman over eight men right now.
>
> One of the nice, satisfying things was to see this one boy and his wife... They are not young people. Well, young. What is young any more? I maintain there are three ages: the old duffers, the young bucks and the people our age. Anyway... as he told it, he said, 'You know something, I never thought when Father Cassedy came and got me out of jail in Bismarck... that I would be here for the 30th anniversary reunion – and want to come back.'
>
> I was so delighted to see the wives and hear them talk about how they had been so anxious to get back to see the place because John or George said this and that about it, had so many things to say about the ranch.
>
> I guess one of the reasons I find myself trying to share with you some of these experiences is because, when you are right there, it is just like when your children turn out good, when you see them as adults and you are proud of them.
>
> You think back to the heartaches and the headaches and you think it was really worth it... Well, I get to see a lot of that. But I would not be able to be here to tell you about it, I would not have such stories to tell if there were not people like you, who are people helping people. People who share.

Closing the deal as any good salesman should, he finally got down to business:

Without you Eagles, I shudder to think where we would be… But because there are people like you, lots of kids are making it in our world today… Because you typify the spirit of unselfishness, the spirit of love that our Savior talks about, of caring about others. You have done it so beautifully, and I cannot help but feel that it has given you a pride in belonging to the Eagles, in being part of a mass of other people who think just like you do, who care just like you do.

Thunderous applause from the thousands gathered at the meal rewarded Father as he prepared to leave the lectern. But, toast mistress Honeycutt and Grand Madam President Ruth Elderbrook weren't quite ready to let Father Fahnlander return to his seat. Instead, they concluded his convention appearance by naming him Man of the Year. The inscription on the handsome, strapping plaque reads: "Presented to Reverend William J. Fahnlander, Humanitarian, Clergyman, Fraternalist. Salt Lake City, Utah, August 1980." Never one to go on about his own accomplishments, not even one so historic, Father Bill kept his acceptance speech short: "What do I say? Thank you. I am humble, proud, grateful. Thank you all" (International Grand Auxiliary Convention Proceedings, 1980).

The "adopted" son of the Past Grand Madam Presidents, Father Fahnlander was the only male ever inducted into the FOE Grand Auxiliary Hall of Fame. Internationally, only three members are instated each year, selected from the membership in 17,000 auxiliaries. This distinction came in 1991, when Junior Past Grand Madam President Kathy Gonzagowski presented the award, her comments recorded within the official proceedings: "This Eagle is so dedicated, not only to this Order, but to a very, very special founding he has in life. He cares so much for children. He cares so much to help so many, that he has friends all across this country and Canada. Tonight, we in the Grand Auxiliary salute you, Father Fahnlander."

Waves of applause and a standing ovation brought the huge banquet hall to life as Father Bill walked to the podium. The inscription on the plaque reads: "Hall of Fame Award presented to Father William J. Fahnlander for dedication to God, dedication to helping youth, and loyalty to the Grand Auxiliary Fraternal Order of Eagles, Cincinnati, Ohio, July 1991."

Another tribute among the many that Father Fahnlander so graciously accepted was the Ruth Meiers Award. Named in memory of Meiers, a

Mountrail County social worker and North Dakota Lieutenant Governor, the award was established to recognize individuals who evidenced the same qualities as Meiers: compassion, dedication, and leadership. Attending the 1996 North Dakota Conference of Social Welfare meeting, Father Bill's honor came the year he celebrated his 75th birthday.

The award was presented for his "outstanding contribution to the disadvantaged of North Dakota." At that particular time in history, Father Fahnlander's involvement with Home On The Range spanned 43 years. "His tenure was marked by his compassion for over 1500 boys who were residents of the ranch, dedication displayed in assuring the continuance and growth of the facility, and leadership as he guided the facility through a time of change. He witnessed a changing social environment that called for major transformation in the program and policies of Home On The Range. The story of Father Fahnlander and Home On The Range is a story of adaptation, of an institution modifying its program to the shifting needs of society. The Home On The Range of 1997 bears little resemblance to 'the ranch' of 1950," the year of establishment (ND Journal of Human Services, 1997). His acceptance speech reflected the qualities that made him such a worthy recipient of the award: warmth, compassion, humility, dedication, and a wonderful sense of humor.

In March 2001, just weeks before his death, Father Bill Fahnlander would be named as one of three Saint Paul Seminary School of Divinity Outstanding Alumni. The award recognizes alumni who have contributed to their vocation in extraordinary ways, having given distinguished service to the Church, while maintaining a supportive relationship with the school. Nominees need also reflect the quality of character that embodies the mission and ideals of the school.

The award was presented posthumously on April 5, during a Mass and reception in St. Mary's Chapel. Accepting the award on Father Fahnlander's behalf were his niece, Mary Jo Norum, and Rev. David Morman, Home On The Range Chaplain and secretary of the board of directors. Father Bill might well have enjoyed picking up this award himself. It was a low-key, matter-of-fact, and to-the-point affair – just the way he liked things when they involved him.

In preparation for Home On The Range's 50th anniversary, Father Fahnlander sat down with journalist and video producer Darrell Dorgan in the chapel at Emmaus Place. The diocesan retirement home in Bismarck, Emmaus Place was the subject of much boasting by Father Bill, who cherished the comradery, convenience, and view from the new facility. He frequently invited out-of-town guests to stop and visit him in his apartment.

A visit nearly always meant a grand tour – including the attached garage where he parked his car, bearing personalized license plates proclaiming "FATHER." The vanity plates were a gift from his niece, Mary Jo, who arranged for them as a Christmas gift. Unsure as to whether her modest uncle would think them too eccentric, she was pleased when he continued to renew them on an annual basis.

Dorgan and Father Fahnlander scheduled several hours to visit about Father Cassedy, the history of the Ranch, and Father Bill's role in the facility's five decades of serving youth. Humble as he was, Father Bill had to be coaxed to divulge much about himself. It was easiest for him to talk about his years in high school and college sports, the boys who had lived at the Ranch, and God.

Winding down the series of questions and answers, Dorgan asked Father Bill to tell about the good times of being a priest. Fahnlander's answer came rather quickly: "The Mass is something very precious. It is receiving the body of Christ, that's the top thing.

"Working with other people does you more good than them. There were times I wanted to beat the tar out of a kid, but the good times outweighed the bad. The Lord said, 'Take up your cross and follow me.' There will be times to carry a cross, but it all has a purpose."

Asked to talk about the trying times, Father Fahnlander paused and gave it some thought: "When you're a priest, you're dealing with people and you're awfully visible. You're trying to do right, but you can't please everyone. Every now and then you get an unsigned letter... There's more than you can get done and you can never close up shop. There are guilt feelings when doing something for myself. You have to learn to let it go.

"Some priests say they don't get affirmation that what they are doing is appreciated. I've not experienced that, not me. So many times people do nice things for me, thoughtful little things and big things. They've been so kind and good to me. A couple years ago for my 50th anniversary I was given a trip to the NFR (National Finals Rodeo). I'd never been there before and never expected to go. It was a big treat for me! The reason I got to go was because I worked with kids and people did this as a thank you. That is an expression that money couldn't buy."

Quizzed as to what he wanted to be remembered for, Father Bill pondered a moment and replied, "Being a caring person."

Granting Father Fahnlander the use of a magic wand, Dorgan asked the kindly, white-haired priest what one thing he would change in the world. Glancing away from the camera's lens and giving it some serious thought, he said: "I'd like to see the world, the society, we're living in be more mindful of the Lord and what we're here for. I guess maybe through all my life I've preached to kids and in parishes 'love of the Lord,' because He loves us so much and we don't respond very well to it. That's what I'd like to see more of. I think that's the biggest problem in our world today, the morality we see around us. There is no standard moral code that is acceptable to everyone. I wish there were and that we'd all live by it."

Dorgan, a veteran newsman and rodeo buff, would relate later how much he enjoyed his time spent with Father Fahnlander during their taping. Sitting in his presence, picking his brain, talking about old times, was a memorable experience for him. As if trying to glean as much as possible from a learned master, Dorgan asked Fahnlander for his best advice. Without hesitation, Father Bill replied, "Live ready to meet the Lord."

Father William Fahnlander lived what he preached, serving as an example to thousands who made his acquaintance. From classmates to parishioners, family members to fraternal acquaintances, he brought a radiance into the world that was enchanting to behold.

A sidewalk stand operated by an enterprising Billy and a neighbor boy. While there is no indication as to what is being sold on this particular day, lemonade was known to be on the bill of fare one summer.
(Photo courtesy of Fahnlander Family.)

CHAPTER FOUR

Growing up "Billy"

Eloise Meyer
Father Fahnlander's Sister
St. Paul, Minnesota

A special memory I have of Father Bill happened many years ago when he was about 8 years old. I happened to overhear him talking to his neighborhood friend, one of the Mowbrey children. They were discussing who should be the manager of their lemonade stand out in the front yard, on the boulevard. Everything seemed so businesslike. This was not just any lemonade stand; they had been going at it for a whole week! At the end of the week there was discussion on how to spend all of their earnings, as they were dividing up all of 11 cents! I never did find out who was the official "manager," but we all know who really was.

If I could send a message to my brother, this is what I'd say:

As children we lived together. We did not always show the love that was growing deep inside. We shared close joy and sorrow. We shared much happiness too. Living through the good and bad times we grew to find we have a love that is special in every way. It is a tender love that is strong today. I could not have chosen a better brother. You are so very special, and I miss you very much.

Margaret Albrecht
Classmate at St. Leo's School
New Port Richey, Florida

I am four years older than Father Bill, so I can say I knew him when he was a little boy. As children we played together. My parents were close friends with Bill's parents. Father Bill gave my dad instructions and baptized him when Dad was in his 50s.

The Fahnlanders lived in northwest Minot. His father had a dry-cleaning business until he died in the early 1930s – during the depression – leaving his mother Mildred to finish raising Bill and his sister Eloise. Mildred moved the family to an apartment above the cleaners.

Father John Hogan took over as a father figure to Father Bill and they became very close friends. Bill grew up to have his mother's quiet and genteel manners and the strict Catholic training of Father Hogan, who led Bill to be a priest.

During those younger years, Bill learned to watch his pennies and worked for his mother. He thought a lot of his mother. When he was ordained, she did not lose her son to the Church, but gained a closer relationship with him.

Father Bill had the ability to make true friends and eventually was ordained and assigned to the Church of St. Leo. He stayed at St. Leo's for a while, eventually being sent to Home on the Range for Boys to replace Father Cassedy.

His parish life changed and he became a guiding light for hundreds of homeless boys. I am sure they never forgot the kindness Father Bill showed them while at the Ranch.

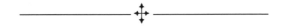

Larry E. Rowan
Classmate at St. Leo's School
Lincoln, Nebraska

Bill Fahnlander and I were boyhood pals from Grade 6 through Grade 12. I would visit his home over Fahnlander's Cleaners for cookies and milk. Bill's mother ran the cleaners, his father having died before I entered Bill's life.

We played on the same baseball team through grades 6-7-8. We went undefeated two years in a row. Bill was an excellent fielder, a good hitter, and fast.

Our school was St. Leo's. When I was a senior in high school, Bill was a junior. We both were starters on a very good basketball team. We won our way through district competition to play in the state tournament in Valley

Young Billy, schoolbooks in hand, stands in the doorway
of the family's dry-cleaning plant on Third Street Northeast in Minot.
The building was constructed by his parents to house their business on
the main floor, with an apartment upstairs where they lived. Photo circa
late 20s or early 30s. *(Photo courtesy of Fahnlander Family.)*

City. It was the first time in St. Leo's history that a team made it to state. We lost our first game.

Father Hogan was both our school principal and our basketball coach. In the summer of 1936 he invited Bill, myself, and Blaine Cook on a summer vacation trip. We drove to St. Paul, Minnesota; Fond du Lac, Wisconsin; Chicago; Detroit; Cleveland; Niagra Falls; West Point; New York City; Philadelphia; Baltimore; Washington, D.C.; and Pittsburgh – back to Chicago and home to Minot. We saw major league baseball teams play all along the way: the Cubs going and coming, Detroit Tigers, Cleveland Indians, New York Giants, Philadelphia Phillies, Baltimore Orioles, Washington Senators, and the Pittsburgh Pirates.

A big deal at St. Leo's each year was the junior/senior prom. When Bill was a senior, his prom date was one of the cheerleaders, Florence Gilmore. Bill's mother was one of the sponsors and I was Mrs. Fahnlander's escort. Two years later, in November 1940, Bill's prom date became my wife. We were married 57 years before she died on October 14, 1997.

During our high school basketball career, Bill and I did a lot of practicing together. One of his favorite shots was dribbling below the basket and feeding the ball to the backboard behind his head with "English." The ball would go straight up, touch the board, and spin into the net. Nobody ever practiced such a shot, so, in March 1938 at the state finals, St. Leo's vs. Stanley, with four seconds left in the game and St. Leo's behind by one point, you guessed it, Bill's shot won the first state championship in St. Leo's history!

The last time I saw Bill Fahnlander was at a high school reunion. It was an all school reunion for St. Leo's and our class's 55th anniversary. Hardly anyone knew me or my few fellow classmates at the Friday night get-together. But, Bill, having been principal at St. Leo's and being extremely popular, was surrounded by a crowd. Everyone wanted to talk to him and had to take their turn. Later he flattered me by suggesting we go to my room and talk over old times.

What a great priest he must have been!

Marguerite (Schaefer) Frank
St. Leo's Class of 1935
Minot, North Dakota

My first recollection of William "Billy" Fahnlander was in 1926 when St. Leo's grade school opened in Minot with six grades. They added one grade per year after that, until they had all 12. St. Leo's Church was the only Catholic parish then and nearly everyone knew each other by name.

Father was a slim young man, very quiet, a friend to all. He was active in sports, especially basketball. His team won the State Class B Tournament in 1938-39.

I remember his mother very well too. She cleaned our St. Leo's band uniforms for free at their dry-cleaning plant many times.

Father was one of Rev. John Hogan's boys who entered the priesthood. He later was principal of the school from which he graduated in 1939.

Over the years we kept in close contact with Father Bill and were his guests at the big two story parish house in Beach. My late husband Ray, daughter Mary, sons Jim and Paul, and I all joined him for supper. While we were eating that night, we saw a mouse run over the back of the davenport. He was caring for Father Joe Adkin's dog at the time. Father Bill and Ray grabbed a broom and dust mop and with the help of the big dog, failed to catch the mouse. Needless to say, no one slept very well that night.

We attended some of his famous rodeos at the Ranch and also visited his mom in her apartment in Beach. He was one of my family's best friends. We kept in touch with him through letters when he moved to Bismarck. In fact, the week before his death he wrote that he would sneak in a prayer during his daily Mass for Ray.

I was unable to attend his funeral service, but have such great memories of him. He was one of the greatest. I think he and Ray are having a good reunion, talking about the years they had on earth.

Marie G. Nistler
Church of St. Mary
Golva, North Dakota

When my husband Don was in the deacon program, Father Blaine Cook would ask us how we were getting along with Billy Fahnlander. It took us a long time to figure out who "Billy" Fahnlander was. He was either "Father" or "William" to us, but *never* "Billy."

Father Cook and Father Fahnlander had gone to high school together in Minot. Father Cook was a senior when Father Fahnlander was a freshman. Father Cook was telling us that one time in high school, the seniors went over to the Fahnlanders' house and rapped on the door, and then went and hid behind a bush. When Billy came out looking, the seniors jumped on him and beat him up. Later we told this story to Father Fahnlander. He said, "No, that is not the way it was," and proceeded to tell us his version of the story.

As luck would have it, Father Fahnlander had a funeral in Golva. Father Cook was con-celebrating and Don was the deacon. Being in the sacristy with the two priests before the funeral and not satisfied to let well enough alone, Don asked Father Cook to tell the story. Father William would jump in and say, "No, Blaine, that is not how it was. Here is the way it happened." So he would start to tell his story and Father Blaine would say, "No, Bill, that isn't the way it was at all." This went on back and forth like this for a while. We were actually glad when it was time for the funeral to start!

CHAPTER FIVE
A Mission to Serve God's People

Rev. Leonard A. Eckroth
The Church of Saints Peter & Paul
Strasburg, North Dakota

I was privileged to have been Father Fahnlander's associate back in 1958 and 1959. He was pastor of St. Michael's in Sentinel Butte (where he resided) and the Mission Church of St. Mary's in Medora. I remember Father Bill for many things, most of all his dedication to the Church and God, his faithfulness to his ministry, and his commitment to young people.

That was a difficult year for Father Fahnlander as Father Cassedy was unable to care for the Ranch following his heart attack and the Bishop was looking for someone to take over the responsibility full time. Father Bill's close friend and mentor was Monsignor Hogan in Minot. Father Bill consulted Monsignor Hogan shortly before Monsignor's death from cancer as to what he should do. Father Bill told me Monsignor advised him to, "Do God's will," which probably meant taking over the Ranch, as the Bishop asked.

There was plenty of stress in his life from working with staff as well as with the boys. One time four of the boys ran away. About a week earlier one of those who ran had his birthday dinner during which he expressed appreciation for what the Ranch was doing for him. "I'm sure those who ran away were acting impulsively," said Father Bill.

We all wondered how he would handle the situation with the runaways. He would not take them back, but referred them all to their juvenile commissioners for appropriate discipline. It was a lesson to the others that running away from the Ranch would not improve their situation.

I remember how every evening during the school year Father Bill would

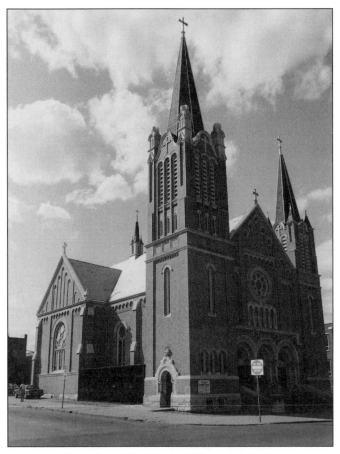

Church of St. Leo, Minot, N. Dak.
(Photo courtesy of Bismarck Catholic Diocese.)

help the boys with their schoolwork after supper. He also did a lot of counseling. The boys occasionally told Father Fahnlander that he was the only dad they ever knew. He was good to the boys, but firm.

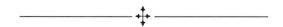

Rev. William Rushford
Retired, Emmaus Place
Bismarck, North Dakota

I don't think Father Bill resented, that from the earliest years of my life with him, I reverently called him "Willie." It was mostly because we shared the same given name of William, the same residence at the start of my priestly life and again at the end of his.

He was well into parish activities when we met, serving as one of the assistant priests at the Church of St. Leo, Minot, and in the capacity as principal of the high school. I stood in admiration of his early accomplishments.

This was my introduction to Catholic education outside of the seminary. Father Bill had enjoyed school at St. Leo's for a good part of his early education, and under the direction of his favorite priest, Monsignor John Hogan. My background in public school and three years in the U.S. Army had me filled with anticipation to enter this "family style" of education.

Much to my chagrin he was soon transferred to be pastor of St. Michael's, Sentinel Butte, North Dakota. This poised him to become successor to Father Elwood Cassedy at Home on the Range for Boys. Having considerable ranching experience, I must admit I was a little envious to see him wearing a black Stetson and cowboy boots. Still, I had to concede he was in every way, perfectly fitted for this new position.

Five years later, to my own surprise, I was transferred to Sentinel Butte as pastor. With this came the opportunity to help at the Boys' Ranch and share some of my knowledge of ranching. When I moved onto other parish work, I enjoyed going back to the Ranch to renew friendships and see the many ways in which Father Bill's hard work was progressing.

For health reasons my retirement came a little earlier than Father Bill's. This gave me the opportunity to welcome him to Emmaus Place, our Diocesan residence for retired priests. He eventually settled in the room adjacent to mine. We both continued to serve the Diocese in various ways.

I used to jokingly refer to the two of us as the "unpaid Bills."

Father Bill's life came to a sudden and unexpected end during the night of March 27, 2001, as I slept unknowingly in the adjacent room. From the flood of condolences and memorials that arrived, I rejoiced to see my friend was receiving his just rewards. Surely all the old hands from the Ranch must be enjoying their reunion with Father Fahnlander. And, I don't think he will be too upset if there aren't any horses there.

May he rest in peace!

Brother Samuel Larson
Society of the Divine Savior
Beach, North Dakota

In 1975 I traveled by bus to Beach, N. Dak., where I was met by Father Maurice Kelch, S.D.S., another Salvatorian and good friend of mine. Father Kelch gave me the grand tour of the Ranch. I also met Father William Fahnlander, the director. I sensed that I had the job even before I made up my mind, but I told them I wanted to spend a few days with the boys before I decided. At that time there were only three counselors for 48 boys. One of the counselors told me I was a godsend.

Father Fahnlander and I discussed the duties. I would work as a counselor, be involved with the sports program, and supervise the work program. A handshake sealed the deal.

After working at Home On The Range for six years, I felt I needed to update my Catholic faith and the teaching of Jesus and the Catholic Church, so I went shopping around the Diocese of Bismarck and beyond. I wanted to stay at Home On The Range. I loved working there and being close to the residents that needed help with their lives. Finally I came across the deacon program and this seemed like it would fulfill my desire for more education in my faith.

There was a drawback, however; I had no desire to become a deacon. I knew that the program would fulfill my needs, so I received permission to attend classes without actually becoming a deacon. After four months in the program, I was pleased with the classes. In one sense they were helping me in my spiritual life and I was getting to know more about the teachings of

Christ and His church. At the same time, I was happy as a Salvatorian Brother.

I was so full of joy I needed to share my feelings with Father Kelch, who was serving in nearby Golva and working with Father Fahnlander at the Ranch. Both priests had a deep friendship in Christ. I visited Father Kelch, who was in the Beach Hospital, telling him all the exciting news about what I was learning in the deacon classes and about the men and women who also attended. Then, out of the blue sky, Father Kelch said to me, "Why don't you become a deacon?"

Before I could answer him, the nurse came in and asked me to leave as they needed to give special treatment to Father Kelch. I left the hospital, but was up in the air about his question. I was determined to go back to the hospital and ask Father Kelch what he meant. It seemed he was waiting for me to ask.

The next day I saw him and my first question was about our conversation cut short the day before. He told me that Father Fahnlander and he had discussed this many times. They both thought I would make a good deacon. I sensed then, that without a doubt, I had been called to become a deacon.

Over the years, as a Salvatorian Brother and a deacon working at Home On The Range, Father Fahnlander always showed me respect and reverence. That is something I cannot forget.

Monsignor Gerald J. Walsh
St. Leo's Grad & Former Home On The Range Board Member
Glen Ullin, North Dakota

Bill Fahnlander and I were both graduates of good old St. Leo's High School in Minot, North Dakota. "Billy," as he was affectionately called in his youth, was some years older than I, so he graduated before I really knew him personally. However, my family used to take our dry cleaning to Fahnlander's Cleaners in those days and so we were acquainted with Mrs. Fahnlander and with Billy's fame as a member of the St. Leo's star basketball team.

When I was in high school, Bill was in college and then in the seminary. There were always some seminarians hanging around the school in the summertime and it was there that Bill and I became friends. He was always kind and friendly to us younger guys. I think that his example, and that of the

Ordination, June 11, 1946, at the Cathedral of the Holy Spirit,
Bismarck, N. Dak. The bishop, Most Reverend Vincent J. Ryan,
performed the sacrament.
(Photo courtesy of Fahnlander Family.)

other Minot boys who were in the seminary and later became priests, had a strong influence on my own vocation.

St. Leo's was a hotbed of priestly vocations in those days. I was number 15 to be ordained from the parish. We were sometimes referred to as "Hogan's Heroes," since Monsignor Hogan had a great influence on all of us.

At any rate, when I graduated from St. Leo's in 1946, Deacon Bill Fahnlander was scheduled to be ordained at the Cathedral of the Holy Spirit in Bismarck, N. Dak. My cousin and classmate, Duaine Frost, and I decided that it would be great to take a couple of our classmates (girls) with us for Father Bill's ordination. It was sort of a graduation outing. We had a chance to visit briefly with Father Bill after the ordination. Later on, after I was ordained, he never let me forget that I attended his ordination with a girlfriend.

After his ordination in 1946, Father Bill was assigned to the Church of St. Mary in Bismarck for a short time and then he returned to his home parish of St. Leo's in Minot. He served there for a long time and was also the principal of St. Leo's School. We became very good friends during those years. When I was ordained in 1955, I asked Father Bill to be chaplain at my ordination. In those days, before Vatican II, it was the custom that each newly ordained priest have a chaplain at his ordination to help him with the Latin prayers as he participated in the Mass with the ordaining bishop. Father Bill thought that he was too young for that position, but I prevailed and was honored to have him with me at that sacred time as I began my priesthood.

Over the years I had the privilege of keeping in touch with Father Bill by serving on many committees and boards with him. My years as a member of the board of directors of Home On The Range will always be remembered because of Father Bill's selfless, tireless, dedicated service to that great institution. He was a man of principle and discipline. He was a priestly priest and a father to countless young men and women who will never forget his smile and compassion. He was a man who was in love with Christ and with His Church, obedient and faithful while always seeking God's will in serving God's people.

Father Bill was an inspiration to me all through the many years of our friendship. I miss him very much and pray for his eternal rest and peace – so well earned and so greatly deserved. Though small in physical stature, Father Bill Fahnlander was truly one of the giants of our diocese. We will never forget him.

Coach Fahnlander explains a technique to players on the St. Leo's basketball team. He coached for two years (1948-1949) while at St. Leo's. Other duties included teaching in the grade and high school and serving parishes in Minot and Glenburn.
(Photo from Home On The Range archives.)

CHAPTER SIX
Tending His Flock

Marilyn Sauer
Church of St. Philomena
Glenburn, North Dakota

I have lived in the Glenburn area most of my life and have fond memories of Father Bill. Father Fahnlander was in Glenburn in the early 1950s. As I recall he lived in Minot and was principal at St. Leo's High School, and was pastor of the Church of St. Philomena in Glenburn and the Church of St. John in Lansford.

In Glenburn he organized a basketball league. This consisted of four teams from the four churches we had in Glenburn at the time. The only requirement to participate was that each player had to attend Sunday services of his choice. Needless to say, attendance at all churches increased! They played every Sunday evening in the city hall which was used for basketball at that time. Many spectators came to watch the games.

Father Bill enjoyed working with the young people and if a team was short a player, he would play – and he was good! He also was a clown on the court. If a team was behind, it was common for him to pass the ball to them even if it was the opponent. He sometimes refereed the game, calling violations on the team that was ahead. The games were always good for a lot of laughs and fun.

Father Bill drove a big car and he was a very fast driver. He would always tell us kids that we had to keep the windows rolled up. Otherwise, Saint Christopher would jump out!

Eleanor Guenthner
Church of St. Leo
Minot, North Dakota

In remembering Father Bill Fahnlander, a small incident comes to mind. As parishioners of St. Leo's, getting to church on Sunday morning was a challenge. My husband Herb and I had four small children and a young baby, and Herb usually worked on Sunday. I was quite often a couple minutes late getting to church. In the homily one Sunday Father Fahnlander, in his gentle way, spoke of coming late to Mass. The gist of his message was that to be on time we needed to prepare, even preparing as far ahead as Saturday night. I don't believe we were ever late again.

Two years ago (1999), Father Bill said Mass at St. Leo's. Our son Bill from Delaware happened to be at Mass with me. Greeting us afterwards, it took but a minute's hesitation before Father recognized us. Even after all those years he remembered us.

Alvin & Betty Tescher
Church of St. John the Baptist
Beach, North Dakota

Father Fahnlander was a dear and beloved priest that we knew for many years. One of his sermons that he had was about when you point a finger at someone, you need to remember that there are three more pointing back at you.

On our 25th anniversary we had asked him to have Mass for us Saturday evening at St. Michael's Church in Sentinel Butte. At the time we were operating the trail rides north of Medora, so we arranged to have the help take care of the business so as many of our family as possible could go to Mass. We all went to the front of the church and in comes Father Kelch. Father Fahnlander had gotten tied up with the dedication of the new dairy barns at Home On The Range and couldn't get away. He came out to the trail ride with the bishop the following day and apologized for missing our celebration.

In March of 2001 our daughter and husband were celebrating their 25th anniversary and asked Father Fahnlander if he could have a Mass for them at the chapel in Emmaus Place where he lived. He said he would, since he had performed their wedding in Sentinel Butte. So, they got an altar boy and reader lined up and went to Emmaus Place. No Father Fahnlander. He had forgotten the Mass. Father Rushford, whom we've also known for years, stepped in and had the Mass for them.

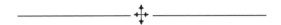

MaryLee Schmitz
Church of St. Mary
Golva, North Dakota

Father William Fahnlander was an outstanding example of the priesthood to my sons when they were young. My oldest son, Jason Paul, was baptized by Father Bill in July 1970. My second son, Jeremy John, had an idea that he'd like to be a cowboy priest like Father Fahnlander.

Father Fahnlander's mother Mildred moved from Minot to Beach so she could be near him. As a nurse working in the local medical clinic, I had occasion to see her from time to time. Father Fahnlander warned me, saying that his mother could be stubborn and had a way of getting a message across. What he was trying to get across to me was that she sometimes had a mean streak.

Sure enough, one time during a visit to the clinic, I was trying to help her onto the exam table. Being the independent lady that she was, she didn't think she needed any help. The next thing I knew she bit my right arm! She got her message across.

Brenda Maus
Church of St. Mary
Golva, North Dakota

From the first time I met Father Fahnlander, I thought of him as a very impressive man. I admired him for his warmth, understanding, and caring nature. He had a genuine concern for the spiritual well-being of all. He was a symbol of dignity and dedication – an inspirational, spiritual mentor for many. He cared to make a difference. I know Father Fahnlander was exhausted many times by all his efforts, but he never let anyone know it.

I will always remember his sermons given with a soft tone of voice. He had a way of having everyone's attention by the way he spoke. During his sermons, I remember sometimes he would gently shake his index finger at you and say, "And ya know…" He never gave a boring sermon that I recall.

He could walk into a room and you just felt his presence, a warm feeling. People were just drawn to him because they knew he cared and cared enough to make a difference. People just adored him for his warmth, understanding, and caring nature. We received a special gift to have him in our community. I felt honored to have this man be the celebrant at our wedding 27 years ago.

Father Fahnlander was a unique priest who will be remembered by the many whose lives he touched. He imprinted upon us an image that will never be forgotten. He is a man I will always admire with utmost respect.

Michelle Hardy
Church of St. Mary
Sentinel Butte, North Dakota

As a kid, I remember Father Fahnlander placing his big, black cowboy hat on his head after Mass. I thought he was sinning when smoking his cigarettes, but always thought God would forgive him more easily since he was a priest!

He was a great friend of the family and always had a joke to tell. My brother Darrell and his wife Renee brought their newborn son to North Dakota from Denver to be baptized by Father Fahnlander 14 years ago. My husband Gary and I had the honor of Father Fahnlander uniting us in marriage July 1, 1988.

When Father Fahnlander said something, he didn't have to say a lot. He could get a message across without many words. During a sermon he could speak in his softest voice and still have everyone's attention. We dearly miss him.

Christine Finneman
Church of St. Mary
Golva, North Dakota

Father Fahnlander touched my heart, as he did many others in the wide, wide circle of those who knew him. His soft-spoken voice could melt anyone's heart, and it did.

He did me a big favor by coming all the way from Bismarck on a Saturday afternoon to say Mass for my 75th birthday. Our regular priest, Father David Morman, happened to be gone that weekend and we had a priest from the Abbey at Richardton filling in.

Father Fahnlander came early and spent the afternoon with us, then he said a beautiful Mass and stayed in my family's midst for the supper meal. What a privilege that was, it was the highlight of my day! After we had eaten, he asked if he could quietly sneak away, he was so humble. He made the drive all the way back to Bismarck that night. He always gave and didn't count the cost.

Karen Wojahn
Church of St. John the Baptist
Beach, North Dakota

The most profound memory I have of Father Fahnlander dates back to 1987. Knowing that he had a heart of gold, and living in a small town, I went to talk to him in my time of need. I wanted to make sure he heard my story *first*.

I made an appointment with him at the parish house. At the time I called, the only thing I told him was that I needed to talk to him – alone. He was a priest so I knew everything I told him would be kept between the two of us. Besides, I was looking for sympathy and who would have such a sympathetic ear as Father Fahnlander?

I sat in his office and told him my sob story: my husband left me and our two children for another woman. I felt like everyone in town was going to be looking and talking about me. I didn't know how to stop it. I just knew that he, having an understanding heart, would have the solution to my problem.

As always, he talked to me with a soft, calming voice, delivering this advice: "My, my, aren't we so vain to think you will never be talked about downtown! Everyone needs to take their turn. Well, be sure to enjoy it because it will be short-lived. Next week they will be talking about someone else. Remember that when you talk about someone, remember how you're feeling today."

That wasn't our whole conversation, but it was the most significant portion. I must admit that when I left I felt somewhat disappointed that a priest would be so insensitive. Yet, it was exactly what I needed to hear.

Marie Hollar
Church of St. John the Baptist
Beach, North Dakota

About a year after Father Fahnlander retired and left Beach, Clara Fakler and I decided to drive to Bismarck. We had to stop for gas on the west end of Mandan, and there happened to be a pay phone there. Since we were close to the Church of Christ the King, we decided to give Father Fahnlander a call. It was almost lunch time so he said we should meet him at the Seven Seas Restaurant just up the hill from where we were parked. We did and after lunch he invited us to come see where he lived.

He gave us a tour of the school, church, and his office. As we entered, we couldn't help but notice his desk. All three of us laughed at the same time. "Yes," he said, "looks just like it used to in Beach!" As busy as he always was, a cluttered desk was the least of his or our worries. I'm sure he got it straightened out once in a while.

I was a sacristan while Father Fahnlander was at St. John's. It was a pleasure working with him. He was so easy-going and appreciative. Many a time he talked about my crown in heaven. I told him I was only looking for a place in God's Kingdom. I'm sure Father Fahnlander has earned many a crown for himself with his holy and pleasant ways.

He was truly a great, kind, and loving priest. God Bless Him.

Hugo & Luciel Kreitinger
Church of St. John the Baptist
Beach, North Dakota

Father Fahnlander was always here for us both, in good times and bad. His love and concern for all was very characteristic of him.

When our daughter Yvonne had major surgery in Denver, Father Fahnlander was in Denver on business for Home On The Range. He went to the hospital to visit Yvonne and gave her a special blessing before surgery.

When our granddaughter Amie died in a car accident, Father Fahnlander was filling in as our pastor after his retirement. Again he was here for our family. His concern and compassion helped us to get through this difficult time.

Father Bill semi-retired in June 1991 and moved to Mandan. His last weekend liturgies included our 50th wedding anniversary Mass and celebration. Once again, he was there.

In addition to being a very compassionate man, Father Fahnlander had a sense of humor! He always had a joke or story for the occasion.

It was an honor to serve on the parish council when Father Bill was our pastor. He will always be in our thoughts and prayers.

Jim & Loretta Tescher
Church of St. John the Baptist
Beach, North Dakota

Father Fahnlander was so much a part of our lives and those of our children. When we heard the news on the radio saying, "North Dakotans are saddened by the loss of a great man, Father William Fahnlander," we were shocked and full of tears. He was such a kind, understanding, and humorous person. We just thought the world of him.

In the earlier years of living on our ranch we had a livable home, but nothing very fancy. I'll always remember what Father Fahnlander said when we were in the process of adopting a child. He put it this way, "Some organizations think a fancy home is so important, but it is the love and caring of a family that is needed the most."

Father Fahnlander presents Jim Tescher with the traditional trophy
rifle for winning the 1965 Champions Ride Rodeo at the
Home On The Range arena.
(Ben Allen Rodeo Photographs, Pasadena, Calif.; from archives of Home On The Range.)

At the 1998 North Dakota Cowboy Hall of Fame induction ceremony in Medora, Father Bill told the story about him and Jim leaving for Cheyenne Frontier Days:

Jim was rodeoing pretty hard then and trying to get his work at home done too, so they decided to leave at 11:00 at night. They didn't know it at the time, but each had the same idea – put in a long day at work and then sleep while the other guy drove. Well, Father Fahnlander drives up in his station wagon with a nice bed made up in the back. Jim was thinking how thoughtful Father Bill was, knowing he'd put in a long day! Jim didn't say much, just crawled into the back. Father Fahnlander did give him kind of a funny look, but got behind the wheel and away they went.

Near Lusk, Wyoming, Father Bill woke Jim up and told him he would have to drive, he just couldn't stay awake any longer. Well, Jim crawled in behind the wheel, but just couldn't keep his eyes open. He pulled it over and slept sprawled over the steering wheel. Father Fahnlander woke him and asked where they were. Turned out they were only about 10 miles down the road from where Father Bill quit driving. They had to drive like heck to get to the rodeo on time! It was a big joke between them after that – going back and forth teasing each other as to how poor a driver the other was!

Elaine Zachmann
Church of St. Mary
Golva, North Dakota

It would be easier to remember when I did not know the kindly gentleman than to say when I first met him. He was one of those people you meet once and it's like you'd known him forever.

On one occasion my husband Harry and I were visiting with him. The topic of singing came up. Harry told Father Fahnlander that he loved music but could not carry a melody so he did not sing, even in church. Father Fahnlander told him that was no excuse. God had given him the voice he had and he should always praise God with that voice. Some time went by, and for some reason Father Fahnlander sat alongside Harry at a church service. Afterwards he told Harry, "It would be better if some people did not sing."

Father Fahnlander and Harry were always sharing a joke. Often he would ask Harry for a new one as he had a speaking engagement coming up and needed some new material.

We shared a joyous occasion when he witnessed the marriage of our son Bern to Mary DeTenancour. Her father Clarence and two of his brothers were brought to the Ranch upon losing both their parents in the early 50s. Father Fahnlander often said that Clarence's children were like grandchildren to him. It was a proud day for him when Mary and Bern were married.

We shared tears when Father Kelch died, for we both had lost a dear friend. Father Fahnlander was there when we needed advice during Father Kelch's illness. There was Holy Week, first communion, and Christmas liturgies that had to be rearranged. In fact, Father Fahnlander filled in for quite awhile until a resident priest could be assigned. Foremost, he was always there, a true characteristic of a friend.

We were in Washington, D.C., upon learning of Father Fahnlander's unexpected death, so we did not get to say goodbye. But then again, friends don't say goodbye. As the saying goes, "The distance between friends is only a heartbeat away."

Judy Clouse
Church of St. Mary
Golva, North Dakota

One Friday evening in May 1980, Father Fahnlander was to speak at the high school commencement exercises at Selfridge, North Dakota. The next morning he was scheduled for an all day Eagles convention in Grand Forks. The following day, which was Sunday, held the routine demands of an 8:30 and a 10:30 a.m. Mass back in Beach.

Father Bill, knowing that he wouldn't be able to drive all those miles in such a short time and still be alert enough to speak at all these special engagements, began looking around for a person who could do the driving for him. He would sleep in the car between each event.

If there was ever something that made this mother's heart sing, it was hearing him ask my son, Kevin Brown, to be that person. What a privilege to have such a wonderful person as Father Bill ask my 17-year-old to make the trip with him! I always figured that Father Bill had an opportunity to share his words of wisdom with Kevin before he took off to college that fall.

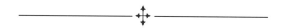

Agnes Schmeling
Church of St. John the Baptist
Beach, North Dakota

I was raised Catholic on a farm east of Golva, North Dakota. My husband Louis came from a very strong Lutheran background. He had not converted when we got married, so the wedding took place in Father Lack's house in Golva. Louis said that he would take instructions and had signed a paper saying so. For a while both of us went to Mass. Though he promised to join the Catholic Church, his family members pressured him not to. Eventually he just quit going, but let me go by myself. Finally it ended up that even I couldn't go to church.

This went on for years and it caused a lot of trouble. Our eight children were caught in the middle. One day I took our five youngest kids and I left home. Louis weakened a lot when he found out how serious I was. He agreed to let me go back to church and started going with me again. Finally some of the kids went too. I had five of them baptized all in one day.

In 1983, we moved from our ranch southeast of Golva to Beach. Louis would go for coffee downtown at Gramma's Kitchen with his good friend, Harold Lang, and Father Fahnlander. Louis took a liking to Father Fahnlander and the two became good friends. I don't really know what happened or what Father Bill said, but Louis ended up being baptized and confirmed in the Catholic Church. Harold was his sponsor. After that Louis never missed a Sunday at church thanks to Father Fahnlander.

Marcella "Sally" Bares
Marillac Manor
Bismarck, North Dakota

I knew Father Fahnlander for many years, but the past 24 years stand out in my mind. When my husband Frank died in Bismarck, we had scarcely returned to Beach from Bismarck when there was a knock on the door. It was Father Fahnlander. It was as if God had sent an angel to help my family.

During these 24 years I became interested in making quilts, not fancy ones, but warm ones for our North Dakota winters. I made one for Father Fahnlander and he was so grateful. We became good friends. It was through him that I started to make and donate quilts to Home On The Range.

While living in Beach, I went to daily Mass. It made my day. Each day after Mass, a group of about eight ladies made a trip to Grandma's Kitchen for a roll and coffee. A few minutes later, here would come Father Fahnlander to do the same. Each morning he would sit with a different group of coffee drinkers. He was a friend to all: Catholic or Lutheran, farmer or businessman. There were none too good or too bad.

I moved to Marillac Manor in Bismarck in November 2000. Father Fahnlander had Mass there quite often. Two days before lent last year, he told me he wouldn't be coming during lent because he had committed himself to helping at the Church of Christ the King in Mandan. But, he said he'd be back the next day yet. I said, "Don't forget I want to hear another story tomorrow." He was a real storyteller.

The next morning after Mass, Father Fahnlander said, "Sally, I have a story for you." I was sitting with several others and this is the story he told us: "The teacher told the class she was an atheist. She asked the students if they were atheists. All hands went up except one. 'Susan, what are you?' the teacher asked. 'I'm a Christian,' Susan replied. 'Why?' asked the teacher. 'Because my father and mother are,' said Susan. 'Well, what if your father and mother were dummies, what would you be?' asked the teacher. 'I suppose then I would be an atheist,' Susan responded."

That's my last memory of him here on earth. I'm sure that he has as busy a schedule in heaven as he had on earth. May he rest in peace.

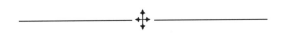

Jayne Hardy
Daughter of the late Richard J. Hardy
Bismarck, North Dakota

It was Christmas Eve 1995 and Father Bill, like all priests, was up to his neck in responsibilities. But he still had time for us, and that's the beauty of this story...

Dad was diagnosed with ALS, or Lou Gehrig's Disease, in the fall of 1994. ALS is a neurological disease that kills the muscles of the body, but leaves the brain sharp as a tack. The information we received painted a dismal picture for Dad's future and that's pretty much the way things went.

It's interesting to see how family and friends respond to one who is dying. Some are quite present, while others find the process too difficult to watch. There were a few who were faithful in their visits, even when conversation was very limited. One such saint was Father David Morman. He came to Dad and Mom's home every Friday for the last several months of Dad's life. It was kind of like "Tuesdays with Morrie," a book that is well worth your time, even if you don't know anyone with ALS. It helps you understand life and death in a different way.

By October 1995, Dad had lost the ability to stand up, walk, or communicate to any degree. Hospice was a saving grace, but even with their assistance, we felt Dad would receive better care in a nursing home. He was so thin and frail. We were afraid we'd break his arms getting him in and out of bed. With heavy hearts we moved Dad to St. Vincent's Nursing Home in Bismarck the day after Thanksgiving.

It was there that Dad spent the last days of his life. Priests and sisters came to visit and pray with him daily. Among them was our longtime parish priest, Father Bill Fahnlander, who was living in Mandan. He would stop in regularly to share a story, a joke, and a blessing. Still, the holiday season was incredibly painful. Dad was suffering and just wanted to go home to his heavenly Father.

We knew that Mass was very dear to Dad's heart, especially during the holidays. Christmas Eve was just around the corner. We thought how awesome it would be if we could celebrate Mass together as a family at the nursing home. But where would one ever find a priest able to say a private Mass on Christmas Eve? Father Bill came to mind right away. We gave him a call to see if he was open to the idea. By the grace of God, he said "yes."

That Mass was such a gift. We prayed, cried, sang, read scripture, and received the body of Christ. Dad even received communion for the first time in quite awhile. Father Bill dipped his finger in the precious blood and placed it in Dad's mouth.

Jesus was very present at that celebration. Jesus was present in Dad. His courage in the face of such awful circumstances was amazing. Others might have chosen the easy way out, but Dad kept his eyes on the crucifix and remembered the suffering Jesus did for us. Somehow that gave him the strength to go on. And Jesus was very present in Father Fahnlander. He had a heart of gold and a genuine love for his parishioners. His love for God and the Church was evident in everything he did.

We'll miss Father Fahnlander's stories and jokes, as well as his presence, at our family celebrations. But even more, the Church will miss an amazing priest. Father Bill Fahnlander was the presence of Christ to us and to all who were fortunate enough to know him.

CHAPTER SEVEN
Raising the Boys

Erv Kessel
Former Beach High School Football Coach
Dickinson, North Dakota

It was October 1962, and I was the head football coach at Beach High School when a worldwide crisis occurred: "the Berlin Crisis." America's Armed Forces were put on ready alert. I remember the day well, for on that day the mailboxes of reserves all over the nation received letters to report for duty.

One of those affected was my neighbor and the head basketball coach, Bob Vooge. Called to serve immediately, he reluctantly reported for duty, leaving his position and creating a void in the coaching staff at Beach High. Staff in those days was very limited and Superintendent Neil Ableidinger asked me to serve until he could find a replacement coach. I accepted, but with no assistants to help me.

Enter Father Fahnlander. I knew that Father Fahnlander had been a very successful basketball coach at St. Leo's in Minot. I also knew that his job and the tasks he was performing at Home On The Range took a great deal of time. I expected to be turned down.

But that wasn't the case. Father Fahnlander, whose load at the Ranch was full, accepted! This astounded me since Father Fahnlander was an extremely busy man, to say the least. Helping me meant giving up a big portion of his day for planning and basketball practice. Remember now, his own Home On The Range staff was very limited in those days. Yet this man, who was so busy and had so much on his mind and such a big load, took on more by accepting this assistant basketball job.

I remember a number of times when Father Fahnlander was called to Beach High School because for some reason or another, one of the Home On The Range boys had violated a school rule: fighting, smoking, or something like that.

I remember his visits: like the father that he was, like the father of that child, showing up to provide support to this child who probably never knew parental support and whose past was loaded with failure and disappointment. His goal always was to help the errant child, to give him a true love, a fatherly love.

Many times when a child did wrong, we talked after the situation passed. I came to know that Father Fahnlander was anguished for the child, but found time to understand and love that child and consequently counsel him – always bearing in mind the child's background, his misfortunes, his miserable life. He showed his fatherly love through understanding and care.

I have never seen such caring from one person for another as did Father Fahnlander for his kids. What love he showed! Each child was important to him.

This was Father Fahnlander. This was his life. He knew no other way. He loved youth and he was a servant. He was motivated with compassion to help youth in whatever way possible.

Over the years we have heard of giving of one's time, talent, and treasure to the Lord. That's what he did, always, and never asking "Why?" Just doing and helping with enthusiasm, in his humble but efficient way and knowing that he did it for the Honor and Glory of God.

1 Corinthians 3:9 says, "We are God's servants." Father Fahnlander was testimony to that.

Name Withheld by Request
Former Boy
Fargo, North Dakota

Home On The Range was my home for 5½ years (1963 through 1968). One day, at the age of 15, I stopped into Father Bill's office because I was troubled. I wanted and needed everyone to like me. I shared this with Father and he gave me some real insight in the reality of life. It went like this:

"Of all the people you will meet in your whole life, 10 percent will like you no matter what you do. They might not like your behavior or attitude at times, however, they will like you. Period. Then there will be another 10 percent who are just not going to like you and it will not matter what you do. They just will not like you. Period."

I then asked, "Well, Father, what about the other 80 percent?" He said, "That's the kicker. Those people won't care either way, so why worry about what others think of you? It's just wasted energy!"

I would like to say I followed Father Bill's advice right away. Reality is, this didn't finally sink into my actions until a few years ago and at times I still catch myself worrying about what others think about me. What a waste of energy! I know, Father Bill was right once again!

Another time, we were trying to get an evergreen to grow in front of the Eagle Hall dormitory entrance. I had tried in vain to get it to grow, but vehicles kept running into it when it was first planted and snow banks piled on it during its first two winters. It didn't have one green needle to be found and I asked Father Bill, "Should we tear it out and make room for something else?" We were standing right next to this tree while we were discussing its fate.

Father Bill told me to leave it there for another full season and if at that time there was no sign of life, then we would get rid of it. Well, guess what? The next season there were a few green needles on the pine tree. Years later an employee sent me a picture of Eagle Hall, and that tree that I almost gave up on was taller than Eagle Hall. What a sight for me to see it in the picture!

I mention this particular story because Father Fahnlander never gave up on me. He never gave up on me when I wanted to quit high school after my freshman year. After I flunked, all he said was, "We are not going to give up on you and neither should you." I did go on to finish high school at Beach and along the way, experienced some things I never thought possible, including winning a scholarship so I could go to college. I was the first one in my family ever to go on to higher education.

In short, I was like that young, beat-up pine tree, and yet because Father decided to give it a chance, it grew and grew. That's what Father Bill did his whole time at Home On The Range. He helped young, behavior problem-plagued adolescents have a second chance to become a real part of the Ranch, the Beach community, and later our own home communities. Thank God for putting Father Bill at Home On The Range to fill in where Father Cassedy left off! It is my opinion that he filled in quite well and I believe the Big Guy Upstairs has already said to Father Bill, "A job well

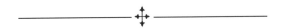

done, my son, welcome home!"

Tom Newman
Former Boy & Educator
Glen Burnie, Maryland

I arrived at Home on the Range for Boys on June 20, 1965. It's difficult to imagine where I may have ended up had it not been for Father Fahnlander.

All the guys referred to our new residence as the "Ranch," our home away from home. Father Bill told me once that his goal was to have all the guys feel as though the Ranch was their home and that we were a family. He accomplished his goal because the guys felt that the Ranch was our home, not just a place to live.

On occasion Father Fahnlander would ask one of the senior boys to accompany him on a trip. One particular time I was invited to go with him to Chicago. Father Bill told me that the trip was a fund raiser for the Ranch sponsored by the Eagles of Illinois. You can't image how excited I was because it was a great honor and privilege to be asked to go!

We set out on our journey in the fall of 1966. I was anxious to go see the skyscrapers up close. I hadn't traveled much outside of North Dakota and it was a big thrill to be going to these new places. We kept moving at a steady pace and the drive itself took us two days. When we arrived in Chicago, I couldn't believe my eyes. I thought the Twin Cities were huge, but Chicago was huge! I'm sure I looked like a star-struck kid staring up at all the tall buildings.

That first night we attended a banquet in our honor at an Eagles Club in the suburbs. It was a very big banquet hall filled to the brim with people. I think I was the only one there under the age of 40. After dinner Father Fahnlander got up to talk and tell everyone about the Ranch, and then I was introduced to the audience. Next a man stood up and announced to the crowd that it was time for the entertainment. The music came on really loud and at the end of the room, a beautiful woman, dressed in a very provocative costume came out on the floor doing a belly dance. Father Bill was seated right next to me and I happened to glance over at him. He leaned over

Appearing in the December 1966 issue of *Eagle Magazine,* the caption on this picture reads: "Father Fahnlander watches pridefully as the boys get ready to leave on the new bus to attend school in Beach, 8 miles away." The bus was purchased with Gold Bond Stamps collected by Eagle Auxiliaries.
(Photo from Home On The Range archives.)

and suggested that I close my mouth and not smile so much. We never discussed the dance again, but I never forgot the experience!

Father Fahnlander was a great humanitarian, and I loved and respected him very much. Had it not been for him, I would not be where I am today. I will be forever grateful.

Mary Bohn
Wife of Former Boy, Lyle Bohn, 1955 –1959
Princeton, Minnesota

"You will have a crown in heaven," are words that I heard so often from Father Fahnlander. I first met him when my husband and I and our children went to Home On The Range for the annual rodeo in 1970. It was the first time the children and I saw the place where my husband had lived for four years, from 1955 –1959. That visit was one of many to come over the years.

The priest in the "10-gallon hat" became a special man to me and my children. Every time we returned to the Ranch, we were greeted by Father Fahnlander with open arms and a big smile. He embraced our children as if they were his own grandchildren. In a way, I suppose they were.

My husband and Father Bill always bantered back and forth during our visits. Father Fahnlander had some advice for Lyle about parenting as we tried to keep track of our five kids running around the Ranch, and Lyle would give Father Bill some new ideas about farming. As the two bantered back and forth with their jokes, Father Fahnlander would wink at me and say, "You will have a crown in heaven" for putting up with Lyle.

After Father Bill retired, we visited with him in his apartment. We talked for a long time about how our children had grown and what they were all doing. We shared with him what we had wanted for our children and for ourselves as we moved on through life; he offered words of encouragement and advice. We always left those visits with Father Fahnlander, feeling renewed and much loved. We miss him.

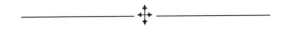

Bernie Keller
Air Force (Retired)
Colorado Springs, Colorado

Father Fahnlander served as superintendent at Home On The Range after I left. He called me well in advance of the Ranch's 25th anniversary celebration and asked if I would speak at a dinner. Those in attendance would be residents, VIPs, and distinguished guests. Father Bill explained that since I was the first boy from Home On The Range to graduate from Beach High School, he thought it would be appropriate for me to tell my story.

There was no hesitation on my part and I told Father Fahnlander I would be humbled, as well as honored, to do so. My experience in making presentations, briefings, and speeches while serving in the Air Force for 20 years, gave me some background on expressing thoughts and feelings, as well as perceptions on a given subject.

The scene of the dinner was the Lincoln Elementary School in Beach; the date, July 5, 1975. The evening was hot and humid, and there were many people in attendance. I was seated at the head table, beside Father Fahnlander. As dinner concluded, Father Fahnlander asked me if I had made key remarks or notes on my cue cards. I told Father Bill I had not prepared any comments on a 3" x 5" card. He said, "You know, Bernie, you're scheduled to talk for 15 minutes about your experiences – good and bad – during the time you spent at Home On The Range (August 1950 to May 1953). I said, "Father, all my experiences were good, therefore, I don't need any reminders to say what I want to express to the audience." Father Fahnlander was still somewhat puzzled as to the content of my talk and the time I would use in making my comments. I spoke for 14 minutes and 48 seconds. The reason I know the exact time is that Father Bill timed me!

My wife Rosellie and I were honored to have spent quality time with Father Fahnlander during the Home On The Range 50th anniversary celebration in August 2000. We attended activities of the North Dakota Cowboy Hall of Fame in Medora, at which Champions Ride was recognized as the Special Achievement Inductee. We also attended the town hall reception, barbecue, and concert for former residents in Sentinel Butte, and the Champions Ride Invitational Rodeo the next day at HOTR. The memories from these experiences and photographs of

Father Fahnlander at these events will forever be cherished by me.
May he rest in peace!

CHAPTER EIGHT
Taking Care of Business

Emma Lievens Kwako
Daughter of Emma and Ed Lievens
Reston, Virginia

In 1950 my parents, Emma and Ed Lievens, culminated a dream of helping troubled boys who otherwise would not have a chance in life. They made a decision to contribute their 960-acre farm near Sentinel Butte, North Dakota, to the Catholic Diocese of Bismarck, North Dakota. The farm became the fulfillment of Father Cassedy's dream and a source of pride and thanksgiving for my three sisters and my family.

I remember well the day that I met Father Fahnlander. It was in the late 1950s. He was warm and gentle, perfect for the care of the boys. By that time Father Cassedy had passed. Father Fahnlander took Father Cassedy's dream, and my parents' working farm, and molded it into a smoothly operating and successful institution. Its reputation grew significantly under his capable managerial and organizational talents.

My parents, three sisters, and I were so happy to see the farm continuing to be a working and productive farm. It was evident that the boys taken in by the Home on the Range for Boys were growing too. They received an education of books and developed a strong understanding of the beauty of God's creation and nature. They were successful at continuing the farming operation.

I was so impressed with how Father Fahnlander was handling the boys and management of the farm. Every year I would come back and see him. Sometimes I had a meal with Father. I loved to hear his jokes and stories. The rodeo was a highlight of our visits and I knew he was instrumental in starting it.

Sadly, in 1962 my father passed. Father Fahnlander bought a ticket and immediately flew to Portland to conduct his funeral and give comfort to my mother and the whole family.

Over the 50 years of Home on the Range for Boys, my family and I had the pleasure of visiting the farm virtually every year. When my mother passed on, Father Fahnlander remembered her by making sure that his regards were conveyed to all of us.

The last time I saw him was at the Ranch's 50th anniversary, a gala affair held in August 2000. He was at the front door of the Sentinel Butte Hall welcoming everyone. It was so good to see him there. Father Fahnlander – he remembered, he cared, he made a difference.

Madge Niece
Former School Teacher
Beach, North Dakota

I knew the boys from Home On The Range from working in the office at Beach High School, so I came to know Father Fahnlander too. One spring day the superintendent asked if I would go out to the Ranch and teach the 7th and 8th grades. I hesitated, but finally said that I'd go.

When it was almost time for school, Father Fahnlander came to talk to me and said it would be a good idea if I stayed at noontime and ate with the boys and staff. I was seated at Father Bill's table and we had many good talks. We talked a lot about religion. I belonged to the Episcopal Church, so we both compared our churches. I got to know when things were well with Father Bill – because he smiled and often told a "Father Fahnlander" joke.

One day at lunch I could tell something was bothering Father Fahnlander, but he said it was nothing. After a long silence I dared to ask, "Anything new today?" He looked very serious and said, "Madge, I think I got two girls in trouble last night."

I suppose my facial expression changed because Father Bill immediately realized what he said. He explained to me that he was phoning long distance to talk to a gentleman on some business and a young lady answered. She didn't connect the gentleman and wasn't very polite, so Father asked her to get someone else on the phone. Another young lady came to the phone, but like the first, wouldn't give any information.

Father Fahnlander finally did get the gentleman on the phone a little later and was explaining to him that he had tried to phone before. He mentioned that the two young ladies were very rude. The gentleman told Father Bill that he would "certainly take care of the matter!" Father Fahnlander thought that the gentleman was probably going to fire the two girls. That was why he was so unhappy.

Winston E. Satran
Home On The Range Executive Director (1986-1997)
Bismarck, North Dakota

My first encounter with Father Fahnlander was on a Sunday afternoon in May 1986. I visited with him at Home On the Range, considering a change in occupations. He was everything I expected: quiet, unassuming, courteous, yet very engaging and somehow captivating.

As I drove out of the driveway at Home On The Range, I told my family, "Don't worry, I'm not going to apply for a job out here." After living in Bismarck, Home On The Range did not look very inviting. I thought the pace of life wouldn't meet the habits I'd acquired after working at the North Dakota State Penitentiary for 17 years.

In the days to come I received several persistent telephone calls from Father Fahnlander. I was beginning to learn of the power of his personality. He told me he was praying that God would change my mind. Over the next few weeks, I slowly became accustomed to the idea that this would be a good place for my family and me.

Father Fahnlander's prayers changed my life in a number of ways. The most significant was learning from him. He told me on many occasions that he never worried. He trusted God. He would relate stories about his early years at Home On The Range, his desk stacked with bills and no idea how he would pay them. Father would say his nightly prayers, go to bed, and have a great night's sleep.

His life was one of faith in God and it brought him a life of peace. Father Fahnlander's great love was Home On The Range; it brought him immense joy. He relished talking with the kids and teasing them with his wry humor. Father Bill was always gentle and kind, and his greatest concern was his fellow man.

He believed in forgiveness and rarely could you detect his disapproval of someone. On the few occasions that I noticed his disdain for someone, I could see that people he did not approve of had the same characteristic: they were self-centered and had extremely large egos. Father Fahnlander was so kind that you would not hear his disapproval, you would only notice that he did not have any positive statements to say about the person. His lesson to all of us was to use discipline when we had judgements about others and to keep our opinions to ourselves, because we are not the judges of our fellow man, God is.

Father Fahnlander had many endearing characteristics, but one of my favorites was his sense of humor. He always had a new story and could deliver those stories to audiences like a master. On one occasion I was asked to be a master of ceremonies at a banquet. On the day of the banquet, I talked with Father Fahnlander and asked him to tell me some new stories. He willingly shared from his bounty and I used them at the banquet that evening. Father Bill was at the banquet, sitting beside a local minister. As they walked out of the banquet, the minister turned to Father Fahnlander and said, "I am surprised at the stories Winston told this evening, I didn't think he was that kind of man!"

The next day Father Fill called and asked me to come and see him. As I arrived at the church, I could see he was busy pacing the parking lot. I immediately recognized from his demeanor that something was wrong. He asked my opinion about the stories and wondered if they offended anyone. I assured him that they were cute, harmless stories that were appropriate and people laughed heartily.

This memory brings us to another dimension of Father Fahnlander. He was continually evaluating himself and his relationship as one of God's messengers here on earth. He never stopped trying to draw himself closer to God and come to know God better.

Father Fahnlander was full of surprises. After suffering a near-fatal aneurysm, he was making a slow recovery in the hospital. One day during a visit, he surprised me with one of his observations: "Winston, this event has taught me a lesson, I need to get closer to God." I was shocked. This man, who spent his whole life dedicated to God, praying his breviary several times each day and living a life of total dedication, thought he needed to do more to reach a closeness to God! It was a strong lesson to me of what the rest of us must do to bring our lives closer to God. Again, Father Fahnlander was teaching us through his own observations of his personal behaviors and habits.

He caused us to think, examine, and change the direction in our lives. This is the story of his life: a man who believed strongly in God, who wanted to know how to better relate to God so that he could fulfill his life's purpose on earth.

We thank God for this wonderful man and how He used him to teach us how a Christian may live his life and remain dedicated and faithful until the last hour.

Marge Grosz
Editor, Dakota Catholic Action
Bismarck, North Dakota

Father Bill Fahnlander was one of the most humble men I ever knew. He was held in such high esteem by people throughout the country, and yet he was as common as an old shoe. When I remember him, two incidents readily come to mind.

The first was when we were preparing an insert for the Dakota Catholic Action commemorating the 50th Anniversary of Home On The Range. Father Bill and Winston Satran sat in my office for a couple of hours doing a taped interview. It was one of the most enjoyable afternoons I have ever spent. One could tell the great admiration these two men had for each other. Father Bill once told me, "If I could have had a son, I would have wanted one just like Winston." What a compliment!

As the two talked that afternoon, it was easy to see that Home On The Range was truly Father Bill's life. He recounted incident after incident with great humor. The history of the ranch unfolded before me that afternoon, but through it all neither of those men took personal credit for its success. What humility! I still have the tape of that interview and it is one I intend to keep.

The second incident I recall occurred just a couple of days before Father Bill's untimely death. He came by my office to inform me that the St. Paul Seminary was honoring him with the Distinguished Alumni Award. He was almost apologetic telling me about it. He was baffled about why he would be selected. (It wasn't hard for me to understand at all.) We visited for over an hour that day. His final comment was, "I don't think it should be a 'distinguished' award, but for someone my age it should be the 'extinguished' award!" The humor and humility were with him to the end.

Don Baertsch
Former Home On The Range Board Member
Beach, North Dakota

It is really hard to be specific about what Father Fahnlander meant to me. He had so many good traits it is hard to say which was his greatest. His compassion for all persons was equal, Protestants as well as Catholics.

I will never forget the day he asked me to serve on the Home On The Range Board of Directors. I said, "Father, I'm not Catholic." Father Fahnlander said, "I know this." I then said, "I am probably not a very good Protestant either, because I don't go to church as often as I should." He said, "I know that too, but I still want you on the HOTR Board."

Serving with Father Fahnlander on the board was a constant honor for me. I will always treasure the many times we rode in my car to Bismarck to attend board meetings. He loved a good joke and could always counter my jokes with a better one. As a reformed smoker, I constantly kidded him about his smoking. He would just smile, open the window a crack, and blow the smoke out the window.

Father Fahnlander was a truly independent person and always did what he thought was right. I asked him if he could witness the marriage of my daughter Sandy in the Catholic Church in Medora. At the time, she was a Protestant. He said "sure" and did so. He also witnessed the marriage of my daughter Dee Ann in the same church. She was also a Protestant at the time of her marriage. Incidentally, both Sandy and Dee Ann have since converted to Catholicism.

No matter what your mood was at the time, you would always be in a good mood after a visit with Father Fahnlander. In all the years I knew him, he always looked at the good side of things and did not have a negative bone in his body.

I know of no individual who has impacted this area (Beach, Golva,

Medora) more or will be missed more than Father Fahnlander. I will sorely miss the smiling face of my friend with the black cowboy hat and black cowboy boots.

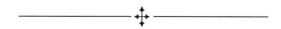

Tammy Gilstad
HOTR Employee (1985-1996)
Beach, North Dakota

It was the Champions Ride Match that introduced me to Father Fahnlander one July day in 1985. We visited at a television station in Dickinson while my brother, Brad Gjermundson, taped an advertisement for the upcoming August Match. Through our conversation, he asked if I would be interested in working at Home On The Range and two days later, I received an application in the mail. Little did I know that our half-hour visit would lead me to 11 years of employment with HOTR and many personal growth opportunities and experiences.

Father Fahnlander's genuine interest in the residents, staff, and guests of HOTR was a special gift. He made himself available to share the joys and sorrows of whomever sought his listening ear and respected advice – wherever he was – in the middle of the parking lot or farmyard, in a dorm, an office, the chapel, or rodeo arena. This carried through to the people he met and knew in parishes, fraternal organizations, and the many places his interests and travels took him. The love and kindness he so willingly shared with others taught great lessons to those around him.

It was a privilege to hear his stories of boyhood experiences filled with challenges and rewards, as well as his respect and admiration for teachers and priests in his formative years. The love and respect he demonstrated for his mother, sister, niece, nephew, and their families was admirable. He took pride in the success stories related to him in letters, phone calls, and visits from boys he guided while at Home On The Range.

Father Fahnlander always acknowledged his many talents and gifts as blessings from God. He also demonstrated tremendous faith in the Lord through difficulties he faced in the different stages of his life. Perhaps the quality I most admired in Father Fahnlander was his obedience to God. He often told of his disappointment in being assigned to serve as the assistant director of the Boys' Ranch when he had aspirations of being a parish priest in a larger community. Yet, he was obedient to the bishop and ultimately to God in his commitment to Home On The Range. God honored his desires of being a parish priest and also gave him many other blessings disguised as challenges, opportunities, and adventures along the way.

My last correspondence from Father Fahnlander came in the spring of 2000 when I faced a serious illness. His letter of encouragement and kindness reminded me again of the tremendous impact he had on so many lives. I am truly grateful to have known this man of great faith, whose lessons of life will continue blessing future generations.

Patrick J. Petermann
Home On The Range Executive Director (1999-Present)
Sentinel Butte, North Dakota

Father Fahnlander was a special man to so many people, not only to those he served in the parish, but also to the boys who lived at Home On The Range and grew up to be men, husbands, and fathers. Hardly a week goes by here at the Ranch without a conversation or story about Father Bill.

Often a former boy will drop in at the Ranch unannounced. They typically spend hours walking around telling stories of their boyhood times at the Ranch. Most of the stories include Father Fahnlander and something he did or said that made them laugh or made them think. Some of the boys state that Father Fahnlander was the only "dad" they had. They recognize that if he wouldn't have been there for them, they are unsure how their lives might have turned out. His dedication to others was overwhelming to say the least. Hundreds of young boys found a loving and nurturing environment that they could call home.

When I was first notified of Father Bill's passing, I was saddened that my time with him was finished. Father Bill was one of my strongest supporters and always had an encouraging word whenever we spoke. He always told me to take care of myself because this business can take its toll on a person.

Some of my fondest memories of Father Bill are of the times we spent together at conventions. We always spoke at the state conventions of the Knights of Columbus, Eagles, and the International Eagles Convention each year. Our ritual was to meet for breakfast and talk about Home On The Range, we'd discuss our goals and visions for the future, and of course, Father Fahnlander always had a joke or two to tell.

I recall my first convention that we attended together up in Minot. I was somewhat unsure of my role, so I asked Father Bill what was expected of me. He put it simply: "I'm the comedian and I'll warm the crowd up for you – the straight guy. All you need to do is be yourself and tell the story of Home On The Range and what we do for the children and families."

After receiving word of his passing, I was responsible for notifying our board members. One of the board members told me that when the position of executive director opened, Father Fahnlander called each and every board member and told them they didn't need to search to fill the position, the right person for the job was already here. It gave me such an overwhelming feeling of support and confidence, this coming from a man who had done so much for so many. I will forever be grateful for his words of advice and encouragement, his humor, and love for others. But, most of all, I will miss his friendship.

Frances Dietz
Home On The Range Employee
Sentinel Butte, North Dakota

Things I remember when I think of Father Fahnlander…

That he witnessed our marriage.

His homilies – he made you feel as if he was speaking to *you* one-on-one.

That no matter how busy or tired he was, he never said "No" when asked to do something, such as going across the country for a wedding or funeral.

His ability to tell a story – remember the one about Isaac and Rebecca?

That just riding in a car with him at the wheel could be a religious experience!

He helped my husband to stop smoking.

That he appreciated a pretty woman – but pointed out he was just looking, like reading a menu at a restaurant.

Our friendship – he was always there for our family.

Clarence J. Fischer
Home On The Range Board Member
Bismarck, North Dakota

On October 13, 2000, we held an evening-long tribute to a wonderful priest. It was billed as a Father Fahnlander Roast and kicked off an endowment campaign in his name benefitting the boys and girls at Home On The Range. Little did we realize, as most of us toasted rather than roasted Father Bill, that so soon we would be putting memories of him on paper. It was such a blessing that we had this event where we were able to *tell him* how great he was, rather than just share memories after he was gone.

We knew Father Bill for 43 years. Memories from those years could fill an entire book. It is with a heart filled with sadness and happiness that we share some of those memories – sadness that he is no longer with us; happiness knowing that he is with our Lord.

Father Bill dedicated his life to helping youth. In doing so he touched not only the youth, but all whom he came in contact with, as he went about promoting help and support for Home On The Range.

Sharing stories was a trademark of Father Bill. You could see him five days in a row and he would always have a new story to share. I remember one evening, at a University of Mary President's Club event in Bismarck, when he was surrounded with people. Knowing that he must be telling a story, I moved in closer to listen.

He was telling the story of a rich man who passes away and shows up at the pearly gates, trying to get into heaven. Saint Peter questions him, "Have you given any contributions during your lifetime?" "No. Well, let me think," he says. "Yes! I gave a quarter to someone one time." Saint Peter excuses himself and goes to talk to the Lord. Soon he comes back and tells the rich man, "The Lord told me to give you your quarter back and then tell you to go to hell."

Father Bill attended the Knights of Columbus annual meetings for many years. Everyone in attendance would look forward to his stories about the youth at the Ranch. They were both heartwarming and heartbreaking. His sharing of success stories made everyone feel that the time and effort put into helping support the Ranch was worthwhile.

His serious report was always intertwined with humor. One year he said that they were hurting for moisture at the Ranch and somebody asked him,

Father Fahnlander spoke at countless banquets and meetings. His favorite topic was always how Home On The Range was changing lives.
(Mosing Studio Photo, Rochester, Minn.; from archives of Home On The Range.)

"You're a priest, can't you do something about it?" He responded, "I'm in sales, not in management."

I served on the Home On The Range Board of Directors with Father Bill for more than 12 years. During that time his love and compassion for the youth in our care was more than evident to me.

Father Bill loved to tell teacher stories. He told one about Mary going up to the teacher's desk, and after telling her that her dad has a flower shop, gives her a bouquet of flowers. The next day little Teresa goes up, tells her that her dad has a candy shop and proceeds to give her a box of candy. A few days later, little Johnnie brings a box and sets it on the teacher's desk. The bottom was all wet and dripping. "Johnnie, what is this?" the teacher asks. The well-meaning Johnnie replies, "My dad has a pet shop. I brought you a puppy!"

I would like to quote Father Bill as he spoke at a Knights of Columbus annual gathering. He said: "I want you to know that we at Home On The Range are honestly and truly grateful for your support. I like to think that if we only helped one of those kids over all these years, it would still have been worth it all. But I like to think it has helped a lot of kids. There's a lot of kids walking around this state, and way beyond, who are doing well and have come back many times to say, 'Hey, I wonder where I'd be if it hadn't been for Home On The Range.'"

To this, my response was, "I wonder where Home On The Range would be had it not been for Father Bill? His dedication, his commitment, his love for the kids is beyond measure. The lives he touched as a priest – doing our Lord's work – have left an indelible mark, not only in the minds and hearts of the many boys and girls at Home On The Range, but in all the parishes he has served."

Father Bill continued to serve until the end. His boots, western hat and suit, and his Dodge Intrepid were always on the move. Many times after his retirement, Helen and I told Father Bill, "Don't forget, you are supposed to be retired. Are you not overdoing it a bit?" His response was always, "I feel good! As long as the Lord allows me, I will continue to do what I love, and that is to serve the Lord in whatever way I can."

My last wonderful memory of Father Bill occurred just three weeks before his passing. The two of us made a trip from Bismarck to Home On The Range for a meeting. I had this rare opportunity to visit with him and share memories of days gone by, the many conventions and meetings we had attended together, and the many experiences he had as a priest. What stands out most about this trip was that we had the opportunity to say a rosary together. I will hold that memory dear to my heart the rest of my life.

Father Bill, we know that you are watching from above as this is being written. Again, know of our thanks for all you did, all the humor you shared, and all the lives you touched in your own unique way. We have been so blessed to have had you as a part of our lives. May you rest in peace. We know your place in heaven is secure.

CHAPTER NINE
People Helping People

Their slogan tells you what the Eagles are all about. They are "People Helping People."

It was the Eagles who started Mother's Day, who provided the impetus for Social Security, who ended job discrimination based on age, who've built training centers all over the world, who raise millions of dollars every year to combat heart disease and cancer. They help handicapped kids, uplift the aged, and otherwise make life a little brighter for people not as lucky and blessed as we are.

They uphold and nourish the values of home, family, and community that are so necessary and it seems so often today, ignored and trampled in society. They are hometown builders. They support police and firefighters and others who protect and serve us. They fund research in areas such as heart disease, kidney disease, diabetes, and cancer. They help raise money for neglected and abused children and for the aged.

They are the Eagles, and they are People Helping People. For over 100 years, they have been leaders in the effort to make the world a brighter and better place for everyone (Fraternal Order of Eagles Web Page, 2001).

Listed among the "Milestones of Eagle Progress" heralding 100 years of Eagle pride is the entry: "1960 – Dedicated Eagle Hall at Home On The Range in Sentinel Butte, North Dakota." While technically correct, the account falls short of communicating the Eagles' involvement in developing the home for neglected, homeless, and troubled children.

The Eagles were there, literally from the beginning. Aeries and Auxiliaries nurtured Home On The Range from its infancy, sustained it through the decades, and continue to provide encouragement and support as it moves into its 52nd year of serving children. Thousands of boys and girls and their families are living happier, healthier, more productive lives thanks to the ongoing efforts of Brothers and Sisters across the United States and Canada.

The Bi-State Aeries of North and South Dakota were the first to recognize the worthy cause advocated by Father Elwood E. Cassedy. Meeting in Deadwood, S. Dak., in June 1949, the delegates at that year's state Eagles convention heard the soft-spoken Cassedy with a New Jersey accent share his dream. He envisioned a home in the country where troubled and homeless boys "could come and work and be taught some kind of a trade, and be made useful citizens."

As the convention was called to order, Father Cassedy had little more than hope of establishing such a facility. By the time it adjourned, he had secured the support of the Dakota Eagles and had received his first cash contribution – $123, raised by a spontaneous passing of the hat.

As valuable as both of these things were, subsequent news coverage resulted in something even more substantial: the home itself. A couple nearing retirement, who could easily have sold their holdings, chose instead to deed the property to Father Cassedy. In July 1950, three boys moved into a remodeled granary on the southwestern North Dakota ranch near Sentinel Butte. Home on the Range for Boys was no longer a dream, but reality.

Lois Nelson
Past Grand Madam President
Fargo, North Dakota

What a privilege and honor it was to have had a great friendship with Father Fahnlander since the 1950s.

Father Bill came to Fargo for a North Central Regional Conference in May 1959. He was shivering in his boots, having the responsibility of presenting the plans for Eagle Hall to a group of Eagles, many whom he had never met before. As those of you who remember, the plans were wholeheartedly accepted.

In the fall of 1959, as I traveled as Grand Madam President for the Eagles, I received word of Father Cassedy's death and Father Fahnlander's taking over the reins at Home On The Range. I had chosen HOTR as my project that year, and with the joint interest from Auxiliaries throughout the jurisdiction, we raised enough money to furnish the dormitory rooms with bedspreads, drapes, and rugs. In addition, we furnished drapes for Father Fahnlander's room and for the library, along with furniture for the entry. This, of course, gave me the opportunity to work with Father Bill and get

Reviewing plans for Eagle Hall at the FOE North Central Regional
Conference - May 1959. Stepping in for an ailing Father Cassedy,
Father Bill had just assumed the role of interim superintendent. With
40 boys crowded into the original dormitory, he felt it imperative to
ask for a larger building, one that included living space. Up until this
point, plans had been for a recreation hall and office combination.
Adding dorm space doubled the cost. Those in attendance agreed that
Eagle Hall should, and would, be built to include dormitory space.
Seated at table: Father Fahnlander; Past Grand Worthy President
Maurice Splain; Grand Madam Vice President Lois Nelson; North
Central Regional President Pete MacArthur; Past Grand Worthy
President Robert Hanson. Standing: Grand Outside Guard Ed Olson;
Home on the Range for Boys Chairman John Ermantraut;
Grand Worthy Vice President Philip Bigley.
(Photo courtesy of Lois Nelson; donated to archives of Home On The Range.)

to know what a kind, mild-mannered man he was. And, oh yes, I might add – humorous.

At one of our Grand Conventions, Father Fahnlander was speaking and put the toe of his boot on the floor, exposing the bottom. The Past Grand Madam Presidents noticed he had a hole in the sole. We immediately decided to adopt him. In one of his comments he said, and I quote: "It is common for a family to have another child every year, but I carry the distinction of obtaining another Mom every year."

For many years I enjoyed taking the current Grand Madam President to the Ranch when she made her visit. Father Bill always gave us a tour of the Ranch and the surrounding sights.

His attendance at our state and international conventions was looked forward to by everyone. He always brought such great messages of the kids at the Ranch and always a cute story.

My husband Don and I had many visits with Father Fahnlander as he was on his way to see his sister in the cities. He stopped on his last trip to see her and we had a two-hour visit with him.

He was a comfort to me when my mother passed away. I was questioning why she had had to suffer. He said, "Christ suffered." This not only was comforting, but food for thought.

We received a letter from Father Bill the day after he passed away. His closing remarks were, "It is supper time so I close quickly. Thanks for being such dear friends."

Ken Reynolds
Past Dakota State President & Past North Central Regional President
Bismarck, North Dakota

In my 30 years with the Bismarck Eagles Aerie #2237, I had enough contact with Father Fahnlander to be one of many who considered him a friend, as well as an Eagle brother.

In 1996, while I was hospitalized with cancer, Father Fahnlander visited me in my isolation room many times and always made my day better. Father Bill had a very serious medical setback as well, but he came to see me anyway. He told me that we would both be okay because "only the good die young." And then, when I lost all my hair, he told me not to worry because they had a new cure: Preparation H. "It didn't make your hair grow, but your head would shrink so what little hair you had would fit better."

Just knowing Father Fahnlander all these years has been an inspiration for me. I will continue to think of him at every Eagles convention that I have the honor to attend.

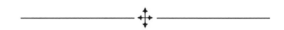

Verna Funke
Past Grand Madam President
Columbus, Ohio

Oh, what to write about this fine man, this man of God… When death hit my family for the first time in the passing of my mother, Father Fahnlander wrote me the most beautiful message that not only soothed me but my whole family.

Father Bill attended our F.O.E. Conventions so many times and he added so much to our programs. I remember one time in particular when he was having lunch with the Past Grand Madam Presidents and officers. I was upset about a few things that went awry, and one more thing didn't work out. It made me angry and I threw my purse – contents flying everyplace. Lois Nelson and Father Fahnlander came over to where I was. Lois picked up the purse contents. Father Bill sat me down, put his hand on my shoulder and in his quiet, soothing voice said, "Verna, nothing is as bad as it seems. This problem, too, will right itself."

I don't know if I ever said a member of the male gender was "sweet" before, but this man that I knew was one sweet, gentle, wonderful man, and certainly had a way with words.

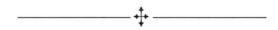

Iola Kaldor
Past Dakota State Madam President
Beulah, North Dakota

Father William Fahnlander was so special to every life that he touched. He was a person that will never be forgotten. Father Fahnlander will live in all of our lives and in many generations to come. It is difficult to write in words the admiration that my husband Al and I felt for him.

We were given the great opportunity of knowing Father Fahnlander through the Fraternal Order of Eagles. We looked forward to his visit, along with the young people from Home On The Range, as we attended the Dakota State Eagles Conventions each year. I remember listening to Father Fahnlander tell of the love he had for these children and how the Ranch had become his life. And, we listened to the children's stories, hearing how they had overcome obstacles because of the contributions made by the Auxiliaries. Those contributions were not only in monetary value, but also love and support shown in numerous acts of kindness.

Did you ever notice how a room, no matter how big, would light up when Father Fahnlander would enter? People from all walks of life knew of Father Fahnlander's work at Home On The Range. We were so honored to have known him even if it was for such a short time. If we had only known him for an hour, it would have been the best hour. Father Fahnlander was loved, respected, and honored by everyone. He gave so much to all of us and asked nothing in return.

I remember my last visit with Father Fahnlander. Judy Sanders, the Fraternal Order of Eagles Grand Madam President, was making her official visit to the Ranch at Sentinel Butte. Patrick Petermann had just presented Judy and me with Home On The Range jackets and we were about to start a tour of the Ranch when Father Fahnlander walked through the door. Father had been at a conference in Medora and came to the Ranch to see everyone.

The love and concern that Father Fahnlander had for the children was always first in his life. Thank you, Father Fahnlander, for sharing your life with us as children of God and also as friends of the Fraternal Order of Eagles.

Bertha Heck
Past Dakota State Madam President
Mandan, North Dakota

Our friendship with Father Fahnlander was one of many wonderful experiences. We visited with Father Bill on our numerous visits to Home On The Range and at Fraternal Order of Eagle functions.

Father Fahnlander, along with my husband Val's cousin, Father Luke Steiner, celebrated our 50th wedding anniversary Mass with us in 2000. It was a pleasure to have him spend the day and evening with our family!

Val and I are both Past Dakota State Eagle Presidents. My president's project in 1972-73 bought a couch and end tables for the chapel entry at Home On The Range. Val's project in 1995-96 was remodeling the library and purchasing books.

Father Fahnlander was always so grateful for anything the Eagles did for Home On The Range. In our days of Eagledom, we were chairmen for the Eagles on several occasions. One such time the past presidents bought Father a suit, and with additional money, the committee decided to get him a pair of boots and a cowboy hat. He was always reluctant to accept gifts, but we put him in the car and took him to the men's store so he could help select his boots and hat. They were presented to him at his visit to the Auxiliary the next day. He was the best-dressed priest in the Dakotas!

CHAPTER TEN
Life with Father

LaVern Jessen
Former Beach High School Coach
Dickinson, North Dakota

Father Fahnlander was a young priest teaching at St. Leo's High School in Minot at the same time I was a student at Minot State. The year was 1953 and I was a member of the Minot State Beaver basketball team.

Each spring it was a tradition at St. Leo's to have the priests play the seniors in a basketball game. My roommate and teammate, Don Wilhelm, was a Catholic and did some coaching at the school. The priests had invited Don to play with them in the seniors' game. I went along with Don to watch.

Prior to the start, Father Fahnlander invited me to play. I said, "Father, I'm a Lutheran!" He said, "That's fine, I'll make you a priest for a day." And he did just that by placing his hand on my head. I got dressed and played with the priests. I don't recall who won the game, but I do remember that Dale Brown, former Louisiana State University Basketball Coach, was a member of the senior team.

After graduation and a stint in the military, I took my first coaching job at Beach High School. Shortly after I arrived, Father Fahnlander was assigned to Home On The Range. I had a large number of boys from the Ranch on my sports team and Father Fahnlander and I developed a friendship that continued until his death. We had many good laughs out of him making a priest out of a Lutheran!

Bill & Jo Ann Meyer
Father's Nephew & Wife
Trempealeua, Wisconsin

From Bill: Some of my fondest memories of childhood revolve around my uncle, Father Bill, and his visits to our family's home in St. Paul. Father Bill had the unique ability to make a young man growing up in the turbulence of adolescence feel special and secure about himself.

When I was approximately 12 years old, Father Bill asked me to come with him to St. Thomas College. At that time St. Thomas had a church on campus which had a basement filled with many small chapels where priests could say Mass. After several attempts at becoming an altar boy – I had lots of problems remembering all the Latin responses – I finally had the opportunity to serve with my uncle at the altar. It was a very special moment.

A few years later Fr. Bill asked me to come out to Home On The Range and spend part of the summer there. I remember taking the Northern Pacific train from St. Paul out to Beach and having Father Bill waiting to greet me at the depot. Back at the Ranch he introduced me to the boys. For the next month I played basketball with the boys, rode horses, butchered chickens, and lived in the dorms with the boys. It was a summer I never forgot.

From Jo Ann: I met Father Bill 34 years ago when I began to date his nephew Bill. When we initially met, Father Bill responded with, "You seem like a nice girl who has a lot going for yourself, so why are you hanging around with my nephew?"

Over the years we had many wonderful times together. Just this past February he spent some time visiting us. Our son Adrian brought his girl-friend Michele over to meet Father Bill. After talking briefly with her he replied, "You seem like a nice girl and you seem to have yourself together, so why are you hanging around with this bum?" His sense of humor brought joy and laughter to many.

Claudia R. Bosch
Third Vice National Regent, Catholic Daughters of the Americas
Dickinson, North Dakota

Father Fahnlander was a friend to so many, including Jim and me. No matter if you saw him at a Catholic Daughter function, the Home On The Range Rodeo, or on the street, he always greeted you with a smile and cheery greeting and took the time to visit.

I remember well the days when Court St. Catherine had him as our guest, along with Father John O'Leary. The two of them would constantly rib one another. We found out a lot about the two of them in the "Good Old Days!"

Jim and I went to the National Finals Rodeo (NFR) in Las Vegas the year Father Bill went, 1996. Despite years of rounding up cowboys to compete in the Home's rodeo, it was the first time he had attended the NFR. We teased him about never seeing him at the rodeos (which of course he had attended) and wondered aloud which slot machine was bringing him luck!

This wonderful man may have been small in stature, even with his cowboy boots and hat on, but he was, oh, so big in heart! I shall always cherish his friendliness, his kindness, and his great love for all mankind.

Richard J. Schall, K of C Council #4894
Past State Deputy North Dakota Knights of Columbus
Minot, North Dakota

Since Father Fahnlander's roots come from Minot, the people here speak highly, and with pride, of him. His family owned a dry-cleaning establishment in northeast Minot and the Fahnlander name is still visible on the side of the building.

I got to know Father Fahnlander through the Knights of Columbus and looked forward to the annual North Dakota Knights of Columbus Convention, knowing that Father Fahnlander would be there and would talk about Home On The Range. We always enjoyed the many touching, and humorous, stories which he told. In the mid-1970s I was the state community activities chairman for the North Dakota Knights of Columbus, which included the honored position of Shamrock Chairman. The Knights have sold lapel pin Shamrocks as a fund raiser for Home On The Range for many years.

It was during this time that I really saw what Father Bill did for the boys at the Ranch and also saw, first-hand, the difference he made in the lives of many young boys. Boys who, for whatever reason, had made some wrong choices and now were receiving another chance.

Several years ago my wife's beautician, who had just married, was telling about her wedding. When my wife asked the new bride where they went for their honeymoon, she said, "Well, our first stop was at Home On The Range." Questioned as to why they went to the Ranch, she said that her husband had spent some time there and he wanted Father Fahnlander to meet his wife, and his wife just had to meet Father Fahnlander! After meeting him, she understood why her husband had so much admiration for him.

This is just one of many stories to be told of how this man reached out to touch the lives of young people. Without making judgments, he loved and nurtured them. Thank you, Father Fahnlander, the world is a better place because of you.

Linda Hawley
Daughter of Gene McCormick, Rodeo Cowboy
Indian Wells, California

I met Father Fahnlander quite by happenstance two years ago in the Ontario, California, airport. We were both waiting to board a flight to Minneapolis. I walked over to him and said, "Father, are you on vacation or business and where are you from?" He said he was returning from an Eagles convention and said he was from Home On The Range at Sentinel Butte, North Dakota.

I told him I was born and raised in Bismarck and that my dad, Gene McCormick, had been inducted into the Cowboy Hall of Fame the previous weekend at Medora, North Dakota. I asked him if he knew my mother Betty Jane. He said he had attended the ceremony and added, "I sat right next to your mother."

Sometimes it pays to be curious and friendly. That made my day and certainly made my mother's day when I told her I had met Father Fahnlander!

Accepting the North Dakota Cowboy Hall of Fame
Special Achievement Award presented to Champions Ride Rodeo in
2000 is Father Fahnlander (center). He is joined by Tom Tescher
(standing, left) and Jim Tescher (standing, right). Kneeling with the
arena flag are NDCHF Director Robert Tibor and Miss Rodeo
North Dakota Robyn Nelson. *(Photo by Jeri L. Dobrowski.)*

Edmund Cassedy
Brother of the late Elwood E. Cassedy
Sun City, Arizona

I remember Father Fahnlander for the many times he made a special effort to visit our home in Sun City, Arizona, while en route to Mesa to visit with his mother. While we were enjoying a pleasant lunch together, Father Fahnlander would bring us up-to-date on the most recent happenings at Home On The Range.

A special remembrance of his great compassion was the time he made a special trip to Jersey City, New Jersey (Father Elwood's birthplace), at the time of our mother's death. He lent his support at a very sad time for our family.

Being able to spend time with him during the 50th anniversary celebration was a rewarding experience for me and the members of my family. We were very fond of Father Fahnlander and will be forever grateful to him for carrying on my late brother's dream.

Mary Jo Norum
Father Fahnlander's Niece
Cottage Grove, Minnesota

Among the many people who touch our lives, there are a few, who by their unique qualities of bravery, courage, or strength of will, transcend the ordinary. We sometimes call these people "heroes." Father Bill was just such a person.

The memory that I will carry with me is how Father Bill embraced his religion and humanity. If I needed to be set straight, I would go to Father Bill. He would do the job. I loved the look on his face when I'd ask a question about a struggle I might be having. The subjects ranged from children, to marriage, and often to spiritual matters.

Father Bill really knew who Christ was. It was as though his whole person would become engaged as he explained the answers I needed to hear. He truly had an intimacy with Christ that I could clearly see. I always came away knowing that what I saw, and who I was with, was *Christ*. I miss Father

Family members gather to help Father celebrate his Golden Jubilee
(50th anniversary) of the priesthood. Those attending the occasion are
(left to right, standing) Jo Ann and Bill Meyer (nephew), Mary Jo Norum
(niece), Ann Norum, Greg Norum, and Father Fahnlander. Seated is his
sister Eloise Meyer. *(Photo courtesy of Fahnlander Family.)*

Bill's hugs, his gentleness, his warm face, his voice.

Father Bill enjoyed the simple things in life. Going to the zoo was a favorite of his. Father Bill also attended many softball and basketball games. Our daughter Annie played basketball and Father Bill would say, "Shoot for the rim." He would sit with our children and practice diagramming sentences. Then there were all the crossword puzzles after Sunday Mass, and of course, the jokes – especially how he'd pretend to refer to cheat notes hidden inside the lapel of his suit coat!

When Father Bill would come to visit, I remember looking out the window as both he and my mother would get into the car. The Fahnlander clan loves a car ride! It was getting hard for both of them the last couple of visits. I knew our time together, and theirs, was limited. I remember saying to myself, "This might be the last time... the only two left in their family."

I miss him sitting at our table and blessing our food. I am committed to teaching our future sons-in-law and future grandchildren about who this great man was.

Father Bill, thank you for all you've been to our family. We miss you very much. Keeping you in our hearts will be easy, and I promise you we will pass your memory on through the generations. You were such a great disciple of Christ, and yet so ordinary at the same time.

You were always, and will always be, my hero. Peace be with you.

Annie Norum
Father Fahnlander's Great-Niece
Cottage Grove, Minnesota

Father Bill was my great-uncle. He was more or less like a grandfather figure and a spiritual leader. He taught me many things that I take with me in my everyday life.

I have fond memories of taking trips out to North Dakota and waiting anxiously for him to come to the Twin Cities to visit. We went out to "cafes" as he would say, to the annual rodeo, and of course, to church.

If I had to pick out just one lesson he taught me, it would be how to pray. On one of the many times Father Bill came to The Cities, it happened to be when I received the Sacrament of Reconciliation. Because he was in town, our parish priest let Father Bill hear my first confession. Afterwards we spent the afternoon together. Being about seven or eight years old, I had many questions about my faith. I asked him, "Father, how do you pray?" He looked at me with his calming eyes and said, "God is your friend. You tell him what is wrong and ask Him for His help, or you confess your sins as you did to me today."

Throughout my life I have questioned my faith and wondered if there is a God. Father always told me it is okay to question faith, but to never forget that God *truly* exists. Father Bill always was patient with me when I had questions and made sure they were answered to the best of his ability.

I will never forget the lessons he taught me, along with all the memories we shared. Although his death left many lives with a loss, I am so grateful that he did not suffer. Many people would agree he did not deserve that.

In closing, I have to say Father Bill was one of the most important and influential people in my life. I am so grateful for having him in my life.

Father Bill, you are so missed. I know we will be together again. I love you!

CHAPTER ELEVEN

Saying Goodbye

Jeanette L. Holm
Church of Christ the King
Mandan, North Dakota

Father William "Bill" Fahnlander became my mentor and spiritual advisor when he moved during his retirement into the rectory at Christ the King, Mandan, my home parish. Our relationship continued when he took up residence at Emmaus Place, Bismarck.

No matter when I called him, Father Bill would have time for me. We shared both happiness and sadness. After a visit with him, which always included reconciliation, my spirits were lifted. My problems may not have been solved, but I was able to face them with hope in my heart. Father Bill had a wonderful gift of always being there when he was needed, with his insightful words and tender manner.

Sadly, I never told Father Bill that he was, in many ways, like a father to me. My earthly father, also named William and called "Bill," had died when I was just 17. Another reason Father Bill and I were so empathic is that much of our lives were spent in the same ministry/profession: his at Home On The Range, mine teaching at the North Dakota Youth Correctional Center where I am in my 35th year.

The morning Father Bill went to heaven, a Christ the King staff member called and informed me, as he knew how close we were. One of the highlights of my life was being asked to lector at Father Bill's funeral Mass. It was there I realized that this humble, wonderful gentleman whom I knew simply as "Father Bill" was a national celebrity known, loved, and admired by thousands. And to think he always had time for me!

I have been truly blessed not only by knowing this gracious man, but also by having Father Bill as my mentor, friend, and father. I miss him so much!

Virginia Marback
Church of Christ the King
Mandan, North Dakota

When I first met Father Fahnlander, it was at our bakery in Mandan – George's Bakery. I went to talk to some ladies in the coffee bar area and as I passed, I saw a man sitting there in a black suit and a cowboy hat. I said "hello" and then sat with my back to him.

Now, anybody who knows me knows that I like to blab. When I looked back and I saw his white collar, I said, "What did I say, what did I say?!" They all laughed and assured me that I hadn't said anything wrong.

I met one of my best friends that day. After that when all the tables were filled, he had his coffee in my office and we talked about everything. He was so easy to talk to. When Father Bill had his 50th anniversary of ordination, I decorated his cake with black cowboy hats.

The day of his funeral there was a table set up at the church with things that had been his. On the table was his black cowboy hat. With a lump in my throat and tears in my eyes, I said goodbye to one of the best friends I ever had.

Father Albert Leary
Homily at the Funeral Mass
Church of Christ the King
Mandan, North Dakota
March 30, 2001

Your Excellency Bishop Zipfel, Your Excellency Archbishop Roach, my brother priests, deacons and religious, members of Father Bill's family, friends in Christ...

Father Fahnlander and I have been friends since that warm summer day 47 years ago, when as a newly ordained priest, I arrived at St. Leo's in Minot to begin work as an assistant in what was at that time the only parish in the city. I was filled with anticipation on one hand and apprehension on the other. I felt a lot of fear and yet, being young, I nurtured great hopes for the beginning of my ministry as a priest. Father Bill Fahnlander was there to greet me and to offer me welcome and support. I felt instantly at home with him. He was a kind and gentle person. I knew he would be the type who would give me encouragement and help me in getting acclimated to a new state, a new city, and a challenging new assignment. We were very different, but I was convinced that he was the kind of man who would be a source of priestly support and strength for me.

He was a priest for almost 55 years when the Lord called him to His Kingdom, probably some time during the midnight hours of last Monday. My opinion never changed and our friendship never waned. I saw Father Bill for the last time just as I was preparing to leave the sacristy to begin the 8:00 Mass here at Christ the King on Monday morning, when he came from the parking lot to prepare for the 9:00 Mass, which he was scheduled to offer. We exchanged our usual pleasant greeting when he sat down in the sacristy to pray and prepare for his offering of the Eucharist.

I loved him very much – this wonderful, priestly friend. I shall never forget him and perhaps those thoughts of mine may even mirror your own as you think of this great priest. He never aspired to honors and always seemed a bit embarrassed when they did come. He had recently been selected as an outstanding alumnus of his alma mater, Saint Paul Seminary, and while he won't be able to be at the presentation ceremony on April 5, he knew that he had been selected and that makes me very happy. He was characteristically modest about it, but deep in his heart, I know he was pleased. He always preferred to stay in the background. He was everyone's Father confessor. He was the shoulder you could always lean on or cry on. He was the one who knew how to listen and share someone else's pain or joy. There were moments in my own priesthood when I needed wise counsel and I drove to Sentinel Butte more than once to sit with him, in that small apartment he had in the original administration building, to share my concerns, worries, and my burdens. He always greeted me with that incomparable smile of which always made me feel that just by coming, I had made his day, and he gave me unselfishly whatever time I needed to get things in proper perspective so I could leave with a lighter heart and a renewed spirit – usually with the problem solved or at least looking a lot more bearable.

The long circle of years that marked our friendship came to a close on Wednesday when I looked down at his now still and silent form, and I vested him in the priestly garments that were a sign of his total identification with the priesthood of Jesus Christ. Of course, I had to see that he had his cowboy boots on too! I am convinced there would have been words at our next meeting if I had forgotten them. Tomorrow morning we will gather again, on the crest of the hill overlooking Home On The Range at Sentinel Butte, to lay him to rest beside Father Cassedy and to pray for the fullness of God's love and mercy for our beloved brother. May he rest there in peace – his tomb greeting the morning sunrise and the first star of evening – until that day of glory and resurrection when Christ the High Priest will summon him from the tomb to share in His resurrection and the eternal glory promised him as God's faithful servant and priest.

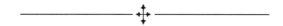

Winston E. Satran
Former Home On The Range Executive Director
Eulogy at Funeral Mass
Church of Christ the King
Mandan, North Dakota
March 30, 2001

Today we are gathered to celebrate Father Fahnlander's life and to mourn his passing as a brother, uncle, priest, fraternal brother, mentor, and friend. Father Fahnlander lived a wonderful life. His life reflected all of that which is good about Christianity. He was forgiving, loving, concerned, kind, and faithful. Father Fahnlander fulfilled many roles in life.

The members of the Fraternal Order of Eagles that are here today also knew him as a celebrity. Each year at the Eagles International Convention, the program would have a list of entertainers and speakers. The list was a who's who of important people in America. There were people like Bob Hope, Danny Thomas, Patti Page, astronaut Alan Shepard, Rich Little the comedian, sports stars from baseball, basketball, football, and boxing; the list goes on.

Year after year, one name stood out – Father William Fahnlander. Father Bill was a celebrity and was known by thousands of Eagles across the nation and Canada. He was always humble about his celebrity's status and it didn't mean much to him. Once he told me an interesting story about his encounter with notoriety:

Father Fahnlander was at the yearly convention, sitting at the head table

Rubbing shoulders with celebrities was one of the perks of the job for Father Bill Fahnlander. In 1965, he was a guest at the International Convention of the Fraternal Order of Eagles, along with Joe DiMaggio.
(Fred R. Stranger Photo, Milwaukee, Wis.; from the archives of the Fraternal Order of Eagles.)

at a banquet. This gentleman kept looking at him and finally acknowledged Father Bill with a nod. Father Fahnlander kept thinking, I wonder who that man is, he looks familiar, I just don't recognize him. After the program the man made his way over to Father Fahnlander and said, "I don't think you know me, Father, but I know you. I'm Dr. Karl Menninger." Now at that time Dr. Menninger was the most famous psychiatrist in the United States and had written a number one best seller *"The Crime of Punishment."* It had been on the best seller list for months. He knew who Father Bill was and wanted to greet him. It is interesting that many national celebrities knew this quiet spoken priest from the plains.

Father Fahnlander's life was remarkable and he grew to enjoy the wonder of it. He reluctantly took the job as superintendent of Home On The Range and told me several times that he grew to realize as time unfolded, that it was the greatest reward of his life. He always marveled at how God worked in people's lives and reflected on his own journey, to demonstrate God's wonderful intentions for each of us.

Father Fahnlander, of course, had a significant impact on many people's lives, none more than the boys who grew up at Home On The Range. Each year in the spring there is a marvelous award given to a notable alumnus of the Ranch. As these men recount their lives, they tell of their personal hardships and how they worked their way to successful lives. They always share credit with those who were instrumental in influencing their success. Every one of them gave their praise to Father Fahnlander. Many of them said he was the only father they ever had. Let's think about it. What a great father he was, always concerned, willing to share ample praise for a job well done. He worked extremely hard to provide for his large family and demonstrated an inextinguishable love for his fellow man. All of these things were true but there was even a more significant reason for all of Father Fahnlander's dedication. It was Father Fahnlander's deep belief that you should give people the best opportunity to seek their own salvation. This was his real mission, his life's work. These were the things that Father Fahnlander talked about when you got close to the reason for his life.

Everyone who encountered Father Fahnlander had a sense of his commitment to God. He wanted to share that with everyone through his own personal touch, through his stories, through his ministry, and most of all, his faithful service to God.

So we are here today to thank God for sharing Father Bill with us for 80 years. We are here to thank God for all of the blessings that he brought to us. We are here today to thank God for Father Fahnlander teaching his brand of grace and humility. Our most important thanks should be to God for teaching us – through Father Fahnlander – what a real Christian is. So we are here to say goodbye to a brother, an uncle, a priest, a fraternal brother, a mentor, and a friend. Thank you, God, for sharing Father Bill with us.

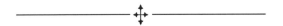

Rev. David G. Morman
Memorial Mass
Church of St. John the Baptist
Beach, North Dakota
April 2, 2001

As I have visited with people this past week and as I look around the church this evening, I see people whose weddings were witnessed by Father Fahnlander; people whom he baptized; the people whom he instructed and brought into the Catholic Church; those he counseled; those whose sins he forgave in the Sacrament of Reconciliation; the sick he visited and consoled; those he prepared for death and buried; those whose house he entered and sat at table sharing coffee or a meal; the people he came to know through Home On The Range, the passion of his life. The list could go on.

This priest encountered people in the casualness of the cafe, the routine of work, the sanctity of the home, and the intimate moments of life. He was one who we imagined would be with us always. His death reveals a truth about our human condition: we are only on this earth a short while, and while we are here, we are to do God's will. For Father Fahnlander, God's will was a mission for him to serve God's people at Home On The Range and in the parish communities where he ministered.

Part of Father Fahnlander's mission in life was to call attention to God and the ways of God — trust, belief in God, the one who holds your life in His hands. During the services in Mandan, Father Fahnlander's niece spoke. She began by asking forgiveness from Bishop Paul Zipfel and Archbishop John Roach (Father Bill's classmate, the retired archbishop of St. Paul/Minneapolis), going on to describe her uncle and saying he was the most Christlike person she had ever met. When she finished, Bishop Zipfel stated, "You don't have to apologize when you meet Christ in someone else."

This statement may say something about our lives — what if others don't see Christ in us — we who claim to be Christian? Certainly, we have a challenge, but God will help us fulfill our mission in life — this is a promise of faith.

As we gather this evening to pray for Father Fahnlander, we entrust him to God. We also pray for ourselves. In our prayer we say:

Thank you, God, for the love and goodness
that has touched our lives through this humble, selfless priest.
Indeed, our lives have been touched by the grace of God
through this gentle man.
We will miss your presence among us, Father Fahnlander.
Please, God, grant healing to our hearts and lives as we grieve.
We renew our commitment to follow Christ more faithfully.

Father Fahnlander had a prayer enshrined on his desk entitled "The Best Way to Live." Attributed to Pope John XXIII, it goes like this:

The Best Way to Live is...
To trust the Lord
To keep peace in one's heart
To accept all things as being for the best
To be patient and good
Never to do ill.

To trust the Lord:
Have a belief that each day and each moment belongs to God and that nothing goes unnoticed in God's eyes. Our lives are upheld by a gracious God, the God who will give us the strength to carry out our mission in life and will grant forgiveness and healing when we fail.

To keep peace in one's heart:
Be mindful of all that one does that does not lead to peace. God has made us to be at peace with ourselves, with one another, and with God. Seek and strive after that which brings peace, the peace and joy that comes from God alone.

To accept all things as being for the best:

It is easier to see that our joys and successes are blessings but this prayer invites us to see our failings, our sickness, our human frailties, our sufferings, even death as being for the best. It expresses a trust in God's providence and care. In God's eyes nothing is lost or neglected.

To be patient and good:

Give the benefit of the doubt to others and take time for one another. One of the greatest blessings we can share with others is the gift of time—our very lives. We are called to be a blessing for one another and the world in which we live.

Never to do ill:

Never, never, never to do ill. Even in our anger, when we are hurt, we are called not to take it out on someone else. At these times we need to pray more fervently for the grace to not allow our difficulties and hurts to embitter us, but that they may shape our lives to trust ever more deeply in mercy and forgiveness as the way to life

Finally, in our prayer, we have another request, and, I believe we are not presumptuous when we say, "Saint William, pray for us."

Joanne Rott
FOE Past Grand Madam President
Grand Auxiliary Memorial Service Eulogy
Fraternal Order of Eagles International Convention
Louisville, Kentucky
August 5, 2001

Father Fahnlander was born February 27, 1921, in Minot, N. Dak. He attended school at St. Leo's in Minot, graduating with a bachelor of arts degree in 1943 from St. John's University, Collegeville, Minn. He then attended Saint Paul Seminary in St. Paul, Minn. Father Fahnlander was ordained in Bismarck, N. Dak., June 11, 1946. He served parishes in

Bismarck, Minot, and Glenburn, N. Dak.

He came to Sentinel Butte and Medora in 1955. At that time he became assistant superintendent at Home On The Range. Father Bill wasn't so sure about coming to the ranch, but Father Cassedy needed him and his talent to help with the ranch as Father Cassedy was ill. And in October of 1959, Father Fahnlander was appointed superintendent at the ranch.

In 1979 the board hired an executive director for Home On The Range and Father Bill served as chaplain. Upon his retirement in 1991, Father Fahnlander was named superintendent emeritus for the ranch, and he continued to serve as a board member. He is survived by one sister, one niece and one nephew.

The Past Grand Madam Presidents have lost their beloved "adopted son." And we will all miss our hugs as we greeted Father at convention. Father Fahnlander was a priest for almost 55 years. He never walked away from a challenge or a calling. Father Fahnlander will be missed by all the children, past and present, who came to the ranch for guidance. He will also be missed by all the people whose lives he has touched. He was a kind and gentle person. This spring he was selected as an outstanding alumnus of the alma mater, the Saint Paul Seminary. Although Father Bill passed away March 26, 2001, he knew he had been selected for the award.

At a memorial Mass on April 2, 2001, Father David Morman told of a prayer enshrined on Father Fahnlander's desk entitled "The Best Way to Live." The prayer is attributed to Pope John XXII and goes, "The best way to live is: to trust the Lord to keep peace in one's heart, to accept all things as being for the best, to be patient and good, never to do ill."

Father Fahnlander will truly be missed by so many people, in so many ways, but it is up to those who knew him to keep him alive in their hearts. Keep his dreams alive and his belief that our troubled youth are worth our time and dedication.

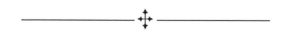

Diane Taylor Szudera
Home On The Range Employee
Beach, North Dakota

As you turn north at Exit 7 on Interstate 94, you can't help but notice the large white cross on a hill a half-mile ahead. This prairie hill, covered with scoria rock, sagebrush, cactus, and native grasses, is lovingly called Father Cassedy Hill. The top of this hill is the final resting place of Father Elwood Cassedy and Father William Fahnlander, two notable men who shared a common cause: serving troubled children.

Those who worked or lived with Father Fahnlander at Home On The Range feel honored to have this gentle spirit buried on the Ranch grounds. Although I believe that Father Fahnlander would be watching over his beloved Ranch no matter where he was buried, there is something special about having his grave close by.

One of my favorite pictures of Father Fahnlander is the one where he is at the top of Father Cassedy Hill, respectfully gazing at Father Cassedy's tomb. The view from the hill is spectacular: an endless expanse of rolling hills, grass waving in the wind, red scoria roads crisscrossing the landscape, and the majestic Sentinel Butte in the distance.

I have heard that when Father Fahnlander lived at Home On The Range, he would go up to Father Cassedy's grave to pray. I imagine he favored that spot not only for the serenity one feels when up there, but also because he could keep an eye on the kids. You can see the entire Ranch from the top of the hill.

I was fortunate to have known and worked with Father Fahnlander for 18 years. His sense of humor, his love for the boys and girls at Home On The Range, and his faith in his fellow man were surpassed only by his love for God. Never have I known such a pure spirit. The memories I have of Father Fahnlander are mental snapshots of his gentle voice to an anxious teenager, his smile on rodeo day as he chatted with the cowboys, and his humorous stories and jokes.

When deciding what to inscribe on Father Fahnlander's tomb, we needed one word that described him. The word needed to reflect how we felt about this wonderful priest, as well as how we thought he felt about Home On The Range and his fellow man. The white marble slab which covers Father Fahnlander's final resting place is chiseled with a large cross, information on his birth, death, and ordination, and the single descriptive word, "Beloved."

This Milt Vedvick photo appeared in the August 1965 issue of *ND Rural Electric Magazine*. The caption read: "Founding of Home on the Range was the realization of a dream long cherished by Father Cassedy. He was superintendent until his death in 1959, following a heart attack. He now lies, as he wished, beneath a marble slab at the top of a high, grassy hill overlooking the ranch. His successor,
Father William Fahnlander, often visits the grave."
Father Fahnlander was buried alongside Father Cassedy. Similar in design and dimension, Fahnlander's tomb lies a short distance to the east (the reader's left). Sentinel Butte may be seen in the distance, on the horizon. The buildings in between are the original dormitory and Eagle Hall.
(Photo from Home On The Range archives.)

Bibliography

Anderson, M. (1983, Aug). Helping boys focus on reality. *N.D. REC Magazine,* pp. 24-26.

Articles of Incorporation (1949, Dec. 28). Legal filing with State of North Dakota.

Baker, L. (1954, July 18). Dream fulfilled in North Dakota. *St. Paul Pioneer Press.*

Bismarck Tribune (1959, March 7). New Assignments for Area Catholic Clergy.

Champions Ride Rodeo Program (1984, Aug). Father Fahnlander recalls past Champions Rides, p 4.

Christensen, M. (1963, July 6). Home on Range testimonial to priest's faith in boys. *Minot Daily News,* p 7.

The Cowboy Chronicle Extra, Special Edition (2001, July) Remembering Father William J. Fahnlander, pp 31-32.

Dakota Catholic Action (1952, Dec). Home on the Range for Boys Is In Its Third Year, p 2.

Dawes, K and Dobrowski, J. (1997, June). Serving Youth in a Time of Change: Father Fahnlander and Home On The Range. *North Dakota Journal of Human Services,* pp 6-13.

Dobrowski, J. (1996, July). Home On The Range celebrates 40th anniversary of Champions Ride Match - Aug. 4. *ND REC Magazine,* pp 8-10.

Dobrowski, J. (1999, Summer). Always At Home On The Range. *Eagle Magazine,* pp 4-6.

Dorgan, D. (1998, Nov). Unedited video interview with Father William J. Fahnlander at Emmaus Place, Bismarck, North Dakota. *Dakom Communications, Inc.*

Eagle Magazine (1958, May). Intensify Efforts to Complete Campaign for Funds To Build Hall for Lads at Boys' Home on the Range, p 22.

Eagle Magazine (1959, Sept). Rodeo Spices Ground Breaking Ceremony at Home on the Range, p 21.

Eagle Magazine (2001, May). In Memoriam: Farewell to a partner and friend, p14.

Fahnlander, Mildred: Funeral Information (1991, Feb. 4). Thompson-Larson Funeral Home, Minot, North Dakota.

Fahnlander, W. (1959, July 27). Letter to Father Elwood E. Cassedy.

Fahnlander, W. (1959, Oct. 21). Letter to L. N. Morrisson.

Fahnlander, W. (Date Unknown). Personal biography.

Fahnlander, W. (1960 to 1987). Home on the Range for Boys annual Christmas letter.

Fahnlander, W. (1963, Dec). A Christmas Message From Home on the Range. Mrs. Eagle, pp 4-5.

Fahnlander, W. (1964, April). Dakota Aeries Notes. *The Minot Eagle* (FOE Newsletter), pp 1,3.

Fahnlander, W. (1966, Dec). Life With Father. *Mrs. Eagle,* pp 4-5.

Father Faber (Undated). *The London Oratory Web Page.* (Cited 2002, Jan). Available at http://www.brompton-oratory.org.uk/page7.html; Internet.

F.W. Faber (Undated). *Favorite Quotes Web Page.* (Cited 2002, Jan). Available at http://home.att.net/~bgray9/Quotes.htm; Internet.

Golden Valley County Pioneers, Bicentennial Edition (1976). St. Michael's Catholic Parish. Sentinel Butte Bicentennial Group, pp 50-51.

Holmberg, D. (1976, July 29). Country priest at home on the range. *The Miami News,* p 5A.

Inductees: Gene Fullmer (Undated). International Boxing Hall of Fame Web Page. (Cited 2001, Dec) Available at http://www.ibhof.com/fullmer.htm; Internet.

Minot Daily News (1938, March 12). St. Leo's Gives Minot First State Class B Basketball Crown.
Minot Daily News (1941, Jan. 9). Here Are The Johnnies From Minot. Miller, T. (1955, Aug. 24). Sentiment Runs High As Parishioners, Friends Bid Goodbye To "Their Father Bill." *Minot Daily News.*
Minot Daily News (1976, May 19). Rev. Fahnlander To Head Harvest For Hunger in N.D.
Mrs. Eagle (1962, Dec). Inspiration Hill Revisited, pp 6-7.
Mulhall, A. (1953, March). Boy's Ranch: Home on the Range for Boys. *Vox Regis,* pp 8-9, 22.

Newsweek, (1951, April 2). Home on the Range, p 74.
North Dakota Governors, Part 4 (1929-1937), William Langer (Undated). *State Historical Society of North Dakota* Web Page. (Cited 2001, Nov). Available at http://www.state.nd.us/hist/ndgov4.htm#langer; Internet.
North Dakotan (1951, Oct). Home On The Range for Boys' Realization of Dream, p 6.
Norum, M (2001). Electronic mail replies to questions for information and clarifications.

Proceedings from the Grand Auxiliary (1980, Aug). Fraternal Order of Eagles International Convention, Salt Lake City, Utah.
Proceedings from the Grand Auxiliary (1991, July). Fraternal Order of Eagles International Convention, Cincinnati, Ohio.

Raymond, B. (1962, Oct. 19). Memory of Father Cassedy still vivid at Home On The Range. *Bismarck Tribune.*

St. Leo's: The First 100 Years (1886-1986) Minot, North Dakota (1986). The Hogan Years, pp 21-26; Interim – Rev. Albert Leary – 1959, pp 40-43; Rev. William Fahnlander, pp 72.
Supplement to the Dakota Catholic Action (2000, Feb). Home On The Range, Working Toward a Brighter Future, pp 1A-8A.

Theodore Roosevelt Rough Rider Award Nomination (2001, Dec). Pp 1-4.
"Two Ton" Tony Galento (Undated). Web Page. (Cited 2001, Dec). Available at http://www.antekprizering.com/galentocollage.html; Internet.

Vedvick, M. (1965, Aug). Home On The Range for Boys. *North Dakota Rural Electric Magazine,* pp 6-8.

Who are the Eagles? and The History of the Eagles (Undated). *Fraternal Order of Eagles Web Page.* (Cited 2001, Nov). Available at http://www.foe.com/history/index.html; Internet.

Yalden, J. (Undated). *Glenn Cunningham.* Keepers Web Page. (Cited 2001, Dec). Available at http://www.pcisys.net/~jjwilson/g3.html; Internet.

A N O R D I N A R Y

D I S C I P L E

O F C H R I S T

T H E F R. W I L L I A M J.
F A H N L A N D E R S T O R Y

To order a copy for yourself or to give one as a gift,
send check or money order, U.S. funds only.
$17.95 plus $2.25 shipping and handling = $20.20 to:

Fr. Bill Book - Dept. IBC
Attn: Rev. David G. Morman
P.O. Box 337
Beach, ND 58621

Profits from the sale of this book are being donated to the Father
Fahnlander Endowment, within the Home On The Range
Foundation. The fund supports religious programming, which is a
vital part of the Ranch's curriculum.

Sorry, no credit card orders accepted.
Please allow 4 weeks for delivery.
ISBN: 0-9718139-0-6

About Our Printer

Finding the right printer for a book is much like choosing a babysitter for your first born child. There's always a worry: will those you've entrusted with the task proceed with the same attention with which you conceived, created, and nurtured the project? What will become of the carefully chosen words and photos once they leave your hands and disappear inside the printing plant?

Our preprinting jitters were soothed once we found Fine Print of Grand Forks, Inc. Don and JoAnn Kuntz and their staff have been a pleasure to work with. But, this doesn't come as a great surprise. Their rapport and craftsmanship were recommended to us by Dr. Edward Keller, Dickinson. Dr. Keller's book, "My Mother's Apron," was brought to life at Fine Print.

Father Fahnlander spent his life helping others start over and make the best of what life had dealt them. The Kuntz family and employees of Fine Print know all too well about starting over. Their business was consumed in the April 1997 flood that devastated much of downtown Grand Forks. Don and JoAnn considered themselves fortunate to have only the basement of their home flooded. The main floor escaped damage, just barely.

At first Don was ready to quit and walk away. The only piece of salvageable equipment was a forklift; everything else was damaged beyond use. A former business partner urged him to reconsider. Six months from the day their livelihood was swallowed by the Red River, Fine Print opened for business in a new plant—away from the river's edge.

There were detours and obstacles along the way. Fine Print operated out of borrowed office space with the barest of business essentials. Don painstakingly acquired used equipment from across the country to replace that left rusting in the scrap heap. Employees accustomed to printing went to work helping build the new plant. Business has been good since the flood and they've outgrown their quarters. At the time of this writing, Don is planning on expanding.

We celebrate Fine Print's spirit and want you to know the success story that is written between the lines of these pages.